C000225726

The Seaside Year

Isobel Carlson

summersdale

THE SEASIDE YEAR

Summersdale Publishers Ltd
46 West Street
Chichester
West Sussex
PO19 1RP
UK

www.summersdale.com

Printed and bound in the Czech Republic

ISBN: 978-1-84953-697-4

Substantial discounts on bulk quantities of Summersdale books are available to corporations, professional associations and other organisations. For details contact Nicky Douglas by telephone: +44 (0) 1243 756902, fax: +44 (0) 1243 786300 or email: nicky@summersdale.com.

Contents

A Note from the Author

THE SEASIDE IS a place that evokes palpable memories – be it the crunch of sand in your sandwiches, catching your first glassy wave on a surfboard, finding a jagged shark's tooth among the shingle or simply the smell of ozone in the air. The UK coastline is a treasure trove of different terrains and spectacular vistas and this book will hopefully give you some great ideas for activities to do and places to see.

BEFORE SETTING OUT, always check the tide times, especially if you are going somewhere with limited access at high tide.

WEAR SHOES WITH grips, especially if you're out walking on a pebble beach or cliffs, and take a simple pair of binoculars so you don't miss any wildlife.

DIFFERENT BEACHES HAVE varying restrictions, from the rules regarding the removal of pebbles to areas that are safe to swim and walk, so make sure you read up about these before you go.

HAVE FUN – and remember to record what you see and do at the seaside in the notes pages each month.

January

Wildlife

A TRIP TO the coast may seem unappealing at this time of year, when the sea is squalling and the wind whips up the sand, but on a crisp winter day, the seaside can be a wonderful place for a stroll and a bit of birdwatching. Check the tide times before you go, as many birds will come to forage when the tide is out. Look out for herons, grebes, ducks, Pink-footed Geese, White-fronted Geese, widgeons and waders. It's worth paying a special visit to an estuary, harbour or beach as it's the peak of the season for coastal waterbirds in the UK.

LOOK OUT FOR tube-nosed seabirds called Fulmars along the Pembrokeshire coast and other rocky cliffs around the UK, particularly the coastline of Scotland and its islands, as they search for potential nesting sites at this time.

WINTERING WADERS ARE a common sight on mudflats, estuaries and marshes. On any given day in the winter months you could spot around 30 different species, including Curlew, Ringed Plover, Dunlin, Turnstone, Knot, Oystercatcher and Black-tailed Godwit.

ONE OF THE most identifiable waders is the Pied Avocet with its black-and-white plumage and distinctive curved-up beak. It winters in coastal lagoons, including those in the south-west, south-east and the Exe Estuary, and can be seen foraging for small crustaceans, aquatic larvae and worms.

IF YOU FIND yourself in Cornwall at this time of year, it's worth making a special trip to the Land's End peninsula to spot the pods of bottlenose dolphins that inhabit these waters through to April. The pods can be as large as a hundred dolphins at a time. Watch as they scour the waters for herring, mackerel, squid and other delicacies. This species is also resident in the waters around Cardigan Bay off the Welsh coast and in the Moray Firth of northern Scotland.

MURMURATIONS OF STARLINGS are a spectacular sight at sunset over the sea in the winter months as they form into sweeping cloud-like shapes, like shoals of fish in their thousands, before roosting in trees and derelict buildings, such as Brighton's defunct West Pier. Other places to see murmurations include Marazion Marsh in Cornwall and Newport Wetlands Reserve in south Wales.

BUTTERFLIES MAY SEEM a surprising sight in winter, but on a sunny day they can be seen basking on sun-warmed rocks and old stone walls. Species to spot include Tortoiseshell and Red Admiral.

Beachcombing/foraging

WINTER STORMS CAN offer up all sorts of interesting flotsam and jetsam, which makes winter one of the best times of year for beachcombing. Cuttlefish bones are a common sight – they have a powdery texture and are stark white in colour and therefore easy to spot on shingle. Egg cases that once housed all manner of creatures from whelks to dogfish are also easy to spot. The egg cases look not dissimilar to bubble wrap. Look out for different colours. If they are yellow, there may still be some unhatched eggs inside, whereas the clear cases are empty. Here are some tips for egg case hunting:

- BEFORE SETTING OUT, make a note of high tide so that you aren't caught out by the waves, which can come in at a terrific speed.

- RESPECT THE WILDLIFE and the environment by avoiding disturbing creatures and their habitats, and don't take any living creatures home with you.

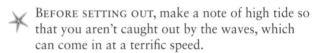

THE BEST PLACE to find egg cases is amongst the seaweed at the high-water mark, or strandline. Use a stick or narrow piece of driftwood to carefully sift through the weed, rather than using your hands as there can be a few nasties in there too!

DRIED-OUT EGG CASES are very light and are blown by the wind across the beach, so look for these against harbour walls, the back of the beach and groynes.

OTHER TYPES OF egg cases to look for are those of skates and some shark species, which lay their eggs all year round. These egg cases are commonly known as mermaid's purses because they resemble little pockets, like small purses with curly tendrils at each corner.

 They vary in colour, but the classic one is dark brown. There is an identification guide on the Shark Trust website, www.sharktrust.org, to help you identify the egg cases that you find.

Seaside activities

New Year's Day swimming

IT'S BECOME A tradition of some of the more adventurous, though some might say foolhardy, among us to take part in a New Year's Day swim in the sea. At this time of year, the waters around the UK are particularly bracing at around 4 degrees Celsius. The swim happens all over the country, and some of the biggest gatherings can be found in Saundersfoot, Pembrokeshire, Barry Island in Wales, the Firth of Forth in Scotland – where the sea swimmers are affectionately known as Loony Dookers – and West Wittering in West Sussex. For many, plunging themselves into numbingly cold water is not enough; they have to go that extra mile and wear fancy dress.

Surfing

SOME OF THE best surfing can be enjoyed in the winter swells, but make sure you're wearing a dry suit and gloves as the water will be freezing cold! Here are some of the UK's best surf spots:

CROYDE, DEVON – this surfers' paradise is the go-to destination due to its fast low-tide waves.

FISTRAL BEACH, NEWQUAY, Cornwall – on the west side of town and with the most amazing structure of a house on top of a rock slap-bang in the middle of the beach, Fistral is a safe bet for surfers as the westerly, south-westerly and north-westerly swells deliver barrelling waves on all tides.

PORTHLEVEN, CORNWALL – close to the Lizard Peninsula, this is one for the experts. It's notoriously dangerous with prevailing winds – often gale-force – coming off the Atlantic. It's considered to have the best right-hand break in the UK, with opportunities for surfing a barrel wave on clean days.

SALTBURN, CLEVELAND, NORTH Yorkshire – this is a great spot for surfing if you're a beginner, with its reliable small swell by the pier.

SAUNTON SANDS, DEVON – around the corner from Croyde, but far less busy, the low-level non-barrelling waves make this beach the perfect destination for longboarding.

SOUTHWOLD, SUFFOLK – a spot for the more experienced surfer, especially on a northerly swell.

THURSO EAST, CAITHNESS, Scotland – this is the premier venue for surfing in Scotland. With snow on the beach in winter and sea temperatures dwindling to around 4 degrees Celsius, this is surfing at its most bracing! Thurso boasts some of the biggest swells and is one for the competent surfer.

THREE PEAKS, LLANGENNITH Beach, Gower Peninsula, Wales – this break is at the northernmost tip of the beach and isn't easily accessible, making it one to head for to avoid the crowds. It has regular surf at low and high tides with an exposed reef that offers some powerful left- and right-handers.

Seaside walks

 THE DORSET COASTLINE, or Jurassic Coast as it's commonly known, is one of extremes – miles of sandy beaches, cliff-backed pebble beaches rich with fossils, cliff paths with a dizzying sheer drop and heathland rich in wildlife. Jewels of the Dorset coast include:

CHESIL BEACH, AN 18-mile shingle beach or tombolo (a strip of shingle or sand that joins an island to the mainland), stretching between Portland and West Bay and joining the Isle of Portland to the mainland. One of the most interesting geological aspects of this beach are the pebbles themselves, because they start big at the Portland end and gradually reduce in size until you reach Bridport, where the smallest can be found.

DURDLE DOOR NEAR Lulworth Cove, an enormous Portland-limestone arch, created by thousands of years of sea erosion. The grasslands on the cliffs are a haven for butterflies in the summer. Look out for the Lulworth Skipper, Portland Spurge and more common varieties such as both species of cabbage white and the Adonis Blue. It's also a popular spot for birds, including Skylark, Raven and Linnet.

STUDLAND HEATH, A national nature reserve near Swanage and the habitat for some rare reptiles. The best time to look out for them is in the spring, when they emerge from hibernation. Lizards and several species of snakes, including grass, smooth and adder, occupy the grassland. Look out for them basking on rocks and the dunes on a sunny day, and look for flashes of the bright green of lizards that are flaunting their colours to find a mate. The heath grasshopper is another rarity indigenous to Dorset and Hampshire.

THE ROCKS ALONG Kimmeridge Bay, formed in the Jurassic period, comprised the sea floor when the waters were tropical. Fossils can be picked up from the beach, and for the truly adventurous there is a self-guided 400-metre-long snorkelling trail marked by five buoys where you can explore different marine habitats. The bay also offers some of the best rock-pooling opportunities around.

Seaside stories

Lighthouses

THESE SENTINEL STRUCTURES are a beautiful and useful feature of the UK coastline, which have for hundreds of years been warning ships to steer clear of treacherous rocks and cliffs, not only with a light but also a foghorn. Some of the finest examples are:

BELL ROCK LIGHTHOUSE, Angus, Scotland – this lighthouse is considered one of the great feats of industrial engineering in the nineteenth century. It's built on an offshore reef and faces a constant pounding by the North Sea, but its masonry was constructed to such a standard that it has never needed replacing.

EDDYSTONE LIGHTHOUSE, PLYMOUTH, Devon – this lighthouse is situated on a small cluster of rocks 13 miles south-west of Plymouth. Its light can be seen for 22 nautical miles. There has been a lighthouse in this location since 1698, but over the centuries it has been rebuilt due to storms, fire damage and erosion, the present 49-metre-high tower having been completed in 1882.

THE NEEDLES LIGHTHOUSE, Alum Bay, Isle of Wight – this classic red-and-white-striped lighthouse lies on the tip of the Needles peninsula, a series of jagged chalk stacks that rise some 30 metres out of the sea. It was built in the late nineteenth century and has walls over a metre thick at its base to withstand the constant pounding of the waves.

WOLF ROCK, LAND'S End, Cornwall – this lighthouse, lying 8 nautical miles off the coast of Land's End, is so called due to the rock's resemblance to a wolf's head, though others believe it's because of the howling wind that whips round it. Completed in 1869, it wasn't until 1955 that it was powered by electricity, having been oil-powered for almost a century.

Martello towers

THESE CYLINDRICAL STRUCTURES, which punctuate the shoreline of the south and east coasts of England, serve as a reminder of military conflict. These impressive buildings, made with brick walls thick enough to withstand bombardment from enemy cannon, and fortified on their flat roof with a single cannon on a swivel-mount, were originally built in the early seventeenth century to protect the coast from Napoleon's navy. A total of 103 towers were built across the south and east coasts, and off the Channel Islands. In the event, the French never made it over the English Channel, and it was not until the advent of the World Wars that these towers proved their worth.

  # Notes

1
....

2
....

3
....

4
....

5
....

6
....

7
....

8
....

9
....

10
....

11
....

12
....

13
....

14
....

January

15
....

16
....

17
....

18
....

19
....

20
....

21
....

22
....

23
....

24
....

25
....

26
....

27
....

28
....

29
....

30
....

31
....

February

Wildlife

LOOK FOR WILDLIFE treasure after the winter storms have passed, as it's an ideal time to go creature spotting. Wait for a clear day and take a walk along the seashore. The newly formed rock pools lined with slippery sea lettuce can be treacherous to negotiate, so make sure you wear shoes with grips on the soles. The most common creatures that you will encounter in rock pools are tiny starfish, jewel-like sea anemones, wriggly shrimps and crabs. Another natural treasure to look for is sharks' teeth, which tend to be black and about 2.5 cm in length – patience is required when searching for these as you sift shingle with your hands.

IT'S HARD TO believe, but there are over 30 species of shark that inhabit UK waters. Basking sharks are the most common and can be seen year-round. They have even been seen in estuaries and are regularly spotted off the coasts of the south-west of England and Wales and around the Isle of Man and the Hebrides of Scotland.

OTHER SPECIES OF shark to spot include the porbeagle shark, which has the more traditional *Jaws*-like appearance with its prominent dorsal fin, grey-white colouring and razor-sharp teeth; and the small-spotted catfish shark, which is flatter in appearance and has a mottled brown skin.

MANY SPECIES OF geese, including White-fronted and Brent, are still prevalent as they overwinter on UK shores before migrating to eastern Europe and Russia for the breeding season. East Sussex, notably the shingle spit at Dungeness, is a popular habitat.

GORSE IS ONE of the most ubiquitous plants on the UK coastline – these spiny evergreens with sunny yellow flowers provide a bit of colour in these dark months and their vanilla scent is heavenly.

Beachcombing/foraging

Collecting seashells

THE ONE THING that is always in abundance on the beach at any time of year is seashells. But how well do you know them? Here's a little guide to the most common seashells found in the UK and how to identify them:

AUGER SHELL – this spiral shell with a sharp point can be as big as 6 cm long. It is ubiquitous on sandy beaches, but is not so common on the south coast.

BANDED WEDGE – these paired shells look not dissimilar to butterflies with their wings spread. Their outer shells are shades of gold, with a delicate purple on the inside. Look for these shells at low tide, half-submerged in the sand, and you may see the creatures that live inside.

COMMON COCKLESHELL – this is one of the most common seashells found around the UK coastline. They are up to 4 cm across with 24 raised ribs and visible raised growth rings. They tend to be pale brown to grey in colour, with off-white insides.

DOG WHELK – this classic snail-shell shape has a pointed spire and a smooth surface, punctuated only by growth marks. The commonest are off-white in colour but others are browns, greys and yellows.

MARINE MUSSELS – these are abundant on many rocky coasts as they cluster to rocks. The shells glisten black but once dried out on the beach, frequently with their two halves intact, are like lapis-blue-coloured butterflies.

RAZOR SHELLS – these are so called because of their similarity in appearance to a gentleman's cut-throat razor. They have two halves, being the former home of a bivalve mollusc, can be up to 23 cm in length and the outer shell varies in colour from reddish brown to purple or pearly white.

SMALL SCALLOP – these bivalved molluscs dance through the water by appearing to clap their shells together, much like castanets. They vary enormously in colour from black and brown through to red, pink and yellow.

TURBAN TOPS – these shells resemble spinning tops, and are only found along the western coast of the UK. They come in all sorts of colours – white, brown, yellow, grey and purple, and some have intricate zigzag patterns on their knobbly surface.

Seaside activities

Message in a bottle

THIS IS A fun activity for children. Find a watertight and robust plastic bottle and write a note, making sure that you include an email address to respond to. Without revealing any personal information, simply ask that whoever finds the message gets in touch so that you can chart how far your message has travelled. Launch your bottle safely when the tide is on the turn, but don't expect a quick response. In 2014 a woman who, as a schoolgirl, had sent a message in a bottle off the coast of Hull was astonished to hear from a couple in Holland, where it had finally washed up, 23 years later!

Let's go fly a kite!

THE BEACH IS arguably the best space anywhere to fly a kite. Pick a day with plenty of breeze, a time when the tide is out and choose a kite that is age-appropriate for all those who will be pulling the strings (an all-singing, all-dancing stunt kite in the hands of a 5-year-old is asking for trouble).

Litter harvesting

TURN A SHORELINE stroll into an 'eco good deed' by filling a plastic bag with any rubbish you find along the way. Better still, sign up for one of the big annual beach clean-up events. Surfers Against Sewage run regular beach-clean events – check out the website: www.sas.org.uk. Join a task force for the day and enjoy meeting new friends while 'wombling'. Get in touch with local Town Council offices to see if they run a regular event that you can join, or visit the *Coast* magazine website: www.coastmagazine.co.uk.

Seaside walks

Dungeness

ON THE SOUTHERN tip of Kent lies one of the largest shingle forelands in the world. As well as being an internationally important site for conservation it is also home to some rare plant and wildlife species, and is one of the best places in the UK to spot unusual moths, beetles and spiders.

APART FROM AN unusual combination of single-storey cottages, two lighthouses, an MoD firing range, a nuclear power station and a nature reserve, the area is largely unpopulated and attracts grass snakes, stoats and weasels, as well as foxes and frogs.

OTHER POINTS OF interest include:

THE LATE FILM director Derek Jarman's house and garden. The house stands out from those surrounding it, with its black-painted shiplap sides and sunflower yellow window frames and door. A John Donne poem, 'The Sun Rising', appears on one side of the house. The garden has been painstakingly designed around sculptures; driftwood monoliths, flint circles and other flotsam and jetsam, including rusty nails and chains, complement the hardy shingle-loving plants.

THERE ARE TWO large, puzzling structures on the beach. One resembles a 'T' shape, the other a diamond shape. They could almost be postmodern sculptures but they have a far more pedestrian use than that. It's a popular area for fishing and before the advent of satnav fishermen had the tricky problem of how to negotiate their way back to shore. These two structures were the answer – by simply aligning the 'T' to the diamond, they had a safe path back to shore.

ANOTHER RELIC WORTH a visit is an unassuming shed dating from the late nineteenth century. It was here, in 1899, that Guglielmo Marconi – the man who invented radio – transmitted the first radio message across the English Channel.

Seaside stories

Shingle

PEBBLE BEACHES, ALTHOUGH not as comfortable underfoot as sandy dunes, hold their own particular fascination; each water-worn stone is a different shape and colour, and the beach almost takes on the appearance of a carpet of jewels when wet from the tide. Some of them are in fact semi-precious stones, although the most common are flint, limestone and granite, having started life by being broken from cliffs, or brought down to the sea by rivers and streams. Here is a list to help you to identify different stones. Always wet the stone before examining it, so that you can see its true colour.

- WHITE WITH GREY knapped edges – this is normally flint, which tends to have 'percussion marks' due to repeated impact against rocks and other pebbles.

- WHITE, AND NOTICEABLY light in weight – chalk, common in the south of England, due to the chalk cliffs.

- BLUE-GREY WITH THIN white lines – these are often known as Cornish pebbles. The blue-grey stone is limestone and the white lines are most often calcite or quartz.

BLACK WITH TINY pockmarks – basalt, which is igneous rock formed from rapid-cooling lava expelled from volcanoes.

YELLOW OR ORANGE, with a glassy appearance – citrine, a semi-precious material.

ORANGE OR PINK, with a glassy appearance – carnelian, another semi-precious stone.

BLACK AND SHINY – jet, most common on beaches around Whitby in Yorkshire.

WHITE AND OPALESCENT – quartz.

ORANGE WITH SPECKLES – amber, which, like jet, is more common on beaches in northern England.

BRIGHT RED AND shiny – jasper, another semi-precious material.

ORANGE-RED WITH POCKS and a grainy texture – man-made brick, which has been eroded from seawalls.

SPECKLED GREY, BLACK, white and silver – this is granite.

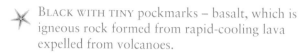

 # Notes

1
....

2
....

3
....

4
....

5
....

6
....

7
....

8
....

9
....

10
....

11
....

12
....

13
....

14
....

February

15
....

16
....

17
....

18
....

19
....

20
....

21
....

22
....

23
....

24
....

25
....

26
....

27
....

28
....

29
....

March

Wildlife

WILDFOWL NUMBERS DROP significantly in March as huge numbers of duck, geese and waders begin the long migration to the Arctic and subarctic regions. Estuaries are among the best places to see migrating birds.

IF YOU VISIT the Skomer and Skokholm islands off the coast of Wales at this time of year, look out for Puffins. There are over 10,000 breeding pairs on these islands between now and the end of August. They nest in burrows that have been previously dug and populated by the islands' wild rabbits. It's one of the most recognisable birds with its black-and-white plumage, brightly coloured bill and red-and-black eye markings. Other places to see Puffins are the Farne Islands of Northumberland, the Orkneys and the Isle of May in Scotland, Alderney in the Channel Islands, Bempton Cliffs in North Yorkshire and South Stack in Anglesey, north Wales.

THERE IS BIRDSONG in the air at this time of year, as birds compete to attract a mate and mark their territory. Yellow Wagtails, Chiffchaffs, Sand Martins and various warblers significantly increase in number, particularly in marshland reserves. Lapwings can also be seen in marshland areas now, and marsh frogs can be heard.

NATTERJACK TOADS CAN be seen on sand dunes, heaths and marshes at a few sites in the south, east and north-west of England and some parts of Scotland, as well as the Talacre Dunes on the Dee Estuary in north Wales. They have brown and green-grey speckles, like the common toad, but they have a yellow stripe down the length of their spine to distinguish them, and they run rather than hop!

SAND LIZARDS ARE rare but have been spotted on sand dunes on the Mersey Coast and parts of the south coast, particularly Studland Beach in Dorset, from March through summer. They tend to be brown in colour but during the mating season the males turn a vivid green to attract a female. They are up to 20 cm in length, nose to tail.

Beachcombing/foraging

Catching razor clams

RAZOR CLAMS ARE as delicious as scallops and are prevalent on coasts throughout the UK. Here are some tips on how to forage for them:

YOU WILL NEED a bucket to put the clams in and a bottle containing seawater to tempt them out of the sand.

SET OUT AT low tide – a spring tide is even better as these are lower than normal. First scan the beach for razor shells. The shells look like an old-fashioned gentleman's razor and tend to be reddish-brown in colour. If you can't see any shells, you won't find any clams!

LOOK FOR A keyhole-shaped hole in the sand – the old-fashioned sort of two holes connected by a slot. Tread lightly across the sand so that they can't sense you.

WHEN YOU HAVE found a hole in the sand, similar to what is described above, squirt seawater into it to simulate the tide coming in.

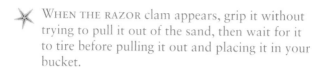

WHEN THE RAZOR clam appears, grip it without trying to pull it out of the sand, then wait for it to tire before pulling it out and placing it in your bucket.

STEAM THEM AS soon as you can, in the same way as you would mussels. Then serve them with garlic butter.

Mussels

THESE BLUE-BLACK SHELLED molluscs are easy to find. They're normally discovered in vast clusters attached to solid moorings, such as rocks, boats and crevices. They are anchored by a byssus thread, or beard, which holds them fast against the roughest seas. They are easy to harvest with a pocketknife and can be collected in a plastic bag or beach bag. Look for the finest specimens, with shiny, undamaged shells that are firmly closed. Bear in mind that you want to maintain the mussel bed, so don't clear it, but pick off a sprinkling of them before moving a step elsewhere to forage for more. Cook them over a fire on the beach and use an empty pair of shells to pincer out the flesh, or take them home and steam them in vermouth or white wine and add shallots, herbs and garlic for a forager's feast.

Seaside activities

IT'S NOT QUITE warm enough to strip off
and sunbathe or to take a dip in the sea
just yet – the sea temperature at this time
of year can be as low as 4 degrees Celsius
– but there is still fun to be had with
some traditional beach games.

Stone skimming

EVER WANTED TO perform the perfect stone skim?
Here's how: look for flat, smooth, palm-sized stones
– the thinner and lighter, the better. Crouch down
low and as close to the sea as you dare. Hold the
stone with your thumb and forefinger and spin the
stone with as much speed and force as you can
manage. The stone needs to remain horizontal to
allow for maximum bounce. You're
considered an expert if you manage
eight bounces or more!

Frisbee

THIS IS A classic beach game but it's surprisingly difficult to master without hitting any hardy sunbathers who don't feel the cold despite the time of year. To throw a Frisbee with precision, follow these steps: point your shoulder towards the direction that you are throwing to – if you are right-handed, point with your right; lefties, point with your left. Place your little finger, ring finger, middle finger and index finger on the curve of the Frisbee, with your thumb on the top. Imagine the Frisbee is a tray with drinks on it – it needs to remain as level as possible. Recoil your arm so that the Frisbee is close to your chest, then fling the Frisbee just before the point that your arm is fully extended.

French cricket

THIS IS PREFERABLE to the traditional game because the only items you need are a tennis ball and a cricket bat, or tennis racket at a push, and you can have as many or as few players as you wish. One person stands with the bat (or racket) in front of their legs. The aim of the game is to hit the batter's legs with the ball, as the legs are essentially the stumps, but not too hard as you don't want to cause any injuries. The non-batters act as fielders, trying to catch the ball as this is another way to dismiss the batter from the game.

Seaside walks

THE YORKSHIRE COASTLINE is amongst the most rugged and dramatic in the UK. Here are some places not to be missed.

FOSSILS ARE ABUNDANT along the North Yorkshire coastline due to its rapid erosion constantly unearthing new treasures. Be particularly careful when hunting for fossils by chalk cliffs and look out for warnings of landslips, which have become more frequent in recent years. For ammonites – the distinctive fossils shaped like a nautilus shell – head for Whitby and Robin Hood's Bay. Other fossils to look for include torpedo-shaped belemnites, which were a type of squid, and bivalves, with their two halves shaped like cockle shells.

FOR IMPRESSIVE CHALK sea stacks and arches, a lighthouse and excellent rock-pooling opportunities, head for Flamborough Head. The bay has a chalk floor with grooves carved out by the sea, which is home to countless starfish, anemones, periwinkles, crabs and fish. At low tide a kelp forest is revealed. Keep an eye on the tide when you're here as it's a steep walk up the cliffs to get off the beach. The bay is home to about 20 interconnecting caves, which can be explored at low tide. The most spectacular of these caves is known as 'cathedral cave', which opens up into an enormous cavern.

THE HEADLAND AT Cowbar Nab, which shelters the fishing village of Staithes, is the ideal spot for viewing seabirds nesting on the cliffs. On any given day you can see and hear Fulmars, Kittiwakes and other gulls as they congregate on the tiny ledges of the cliffs. House Martins also thrive on these rocky cliffs, which may seem unusual, but they build their nests on the underside of the rocks in the same way that they would build them under the eaves of buildings.

Seaside stories

MANY SHIPWRECKS END up on UK shores, although by their very nature they tend to remain underwater. There are a small number, though, that protrude out of the sands at low tide and can be visited on foot.

The Amsterdam, Bulverhythe, between Bexhill-on-Sea and Hastings, East Sussex

THIS SHIP, BUILT in 1748, was 46 metres long and had 54 guns mounted on its upper and lower decks. It was sailing from Texel in the Netherlands to Java, an island in Indonesia, with a cargo of silver, wine and cloth, and a mixture of crew and military personnel, a total of 335 people. It is believed that the crew mutinied and the boat was wrecked in a storm at Bulverhythe on 26 January 1749, whereupon it was plundered by local smugglers, although some of the crew survived and were taken to safety in Hastings.

CHECK THE TIDE times before heading out – it's best to visit the site at low tide in the spring and summer months. Much of the ship is buried in the sand and peat clay of the prehistoric forest that dates from 2000 BC. What is visible is a simple skeleton of well-preserved wooden stumps, which you can walk around freely, but beware of quicksand close by!

March

The Helvetia, Rhossili Beach, Gower Peninsula, Wales

THERE ARE THREE wrecks on this particular stretch of beach, but the most prominent is the Norwegian vessel *Helvetia*, which ran aground in 1887. Its sea-worn carcass is visible at low tide, jutting out of the sand, and can be seen from the clifftops.

SV Carl, Booby's Bay, near Padstow, Cornwall

THIS STEEL-MADE GERMAN sailing ship was wrecked during World War One on 7 October 1917. It had been impounded by the British and was being towed in readiness for the scrapyard, but it came loose from its tow and was wrecked on the beach. It has been submerged in the sand for many years but the winter storms of 2013 stripped its coverings, exposing it for the first time in just under a century. It's a massive structure, where mooring bollards and masts are visible, although time and tide is slowly burying it again.

 # Notes

1
....

2
....

3
....

4
....

5
....

6
....

7
....

8
....

9
....

10
....

11
....

12
....

13
....

14
....

March

15 ....

16 ....

17 ....

18 ....

19 ....

20 ....

21 ....

22 ....

23 ....

24 ....

25 ....

26 ....

27 ....

28 ....

29 ....

30 ....

31 ....

April

Wildlife

DRIFTS OF ORCHIDS start to appear on the grasslands on chalk cliffs now. Look for common spotted and pyramidal orchids, along with northern marsh and bee. Butterflies are also abundant in the grasslands, including Small Skipper, Small Copper, Common Blue, Fritillary and Monarch. Moths to look for include Sand Dart, White Spot, Chalk Carpet and Rosy Wave.

VEGETATED SHINGLE IS home to many types of plant – look for wild carrot, sorrel, dog violet and many types of grasses, including sand couch and marram grass.

ONE OF THE most whimsical marine creatures, the seahorse, can be spotted in waters throughout the UK and Ireland. There are two species indigenous to UK waters: the short-snouted seahorse and the spiny seahorse. They live in shallow water thick with eelgrass, and can be spotted when snorkelling, but they move to deeper waters in rough weather. Studland Bay in Dorset is known to have a colony of spiny seahorses; however, the population has dropped dramatically in recent years due to tourism. The eelgrass beds of the Salcombe-Kingsbridge estuary in south Devon is another place where seahorses have been seen.

April

THE CLIFFS AT Flamborough in North Yorkshire are alive with a cacophony of sea birds at this time of year as they return to breed at its chalk ledges. Gannets, Fulmars, Herring Gulls and Kittiwakes are among the 200,000 birds that make this area their temporary home until September.

HARBOUR PORPOISES CAN be seen off the coast throughout the UK, from Dungeness in Kent right up to the Orkneys. They favour shallow waters where they forage for schooling fish and tend to be a solitary species. They are dark grey with slightly speckled sides and are the smallest of the species, being less than 2 metres long from nose to tail.

COASTAL OTTERS CAN be spotted in Spey Bay, the biggest shingle beach in Scotland, which borders a reed bed and saltmarsh. Normally favouring Alaskan waters, they are attracted by the clean water and foraging opportunities.

Beachcombing/foraging

Seaweed

THERE ARE OVER 650 varieties of seaweed to be found around the UK coast, some of which are edible. Some of the most common and easily identified seaweeds include carragheen, dulse, laver, tangle/oarweed, wracks and sea lettuce.

SEAWEEDS ARE PACKED with nutrients as they absorb and concentrate them directly from the surrounding water. Yet this ability to absorb nutrients also means that they absorb pollutants.

IT IS RECOMMENDED that living seaweeds attached to rocks should be collected, and not harvested from the strandline. Always wash them before eating. Cooking methods will vary according to the individual seaweed:

April

Dulse

THIS PLANT IS delicious eaten raw, after being sun-dried. It can be added to stir-fries and soups, and is traditionally mixed with mashed potato in Ireland. Its dark red to brown fronds are long with divided tips. Dulse is best collected from April to September, found among the shoreline's rocks.

Sea lettuce

THIS IS FOUND in high-tide zones along the shore and on mudflats. It resembles lettuce, hence its name, and is best harvested in spring. It is rich in iron and vitamin C and can be eaten raw in salads or deep-fried to produce a seaweed crisp.

Sea beet

THIS PLANT GROWS on cliffs and sand dunes, and tastes surprisingly similar to spinach and can be prepared in the same way as its domestic counterpart. This broad-leafed plant is the wild relative of Swiss chard and beetroot and can be eaten raw in salads or wilted with butter.

Seaside activities

Crabbing

THIS IS A really fun activity that all the family can enjoy. Be warned: it can get very competitive! There are crabbing holes in many locations on the coast, West Wittering in West Sussex and Looe Millpond in Cornwall to name just a couple, but crabbing can also be done by harbour walls and other places where the water is calm. Here are some dos and don'ts for successful crabbing:

 BEFORE SETTING OUT, brush up on the laws attached to catching crabs, as there are size restrictions, and a couple of species, namely the spider and green crabs, are protected. For more information look at www.mba.ac.uk.

 START CRABBING JUST as the tide is beginning to rise, as crabs tend to bury themselves in the sand when the tide is going out.

 THE FAVOURED BAIT for crabbing is raw bacon rind carefully tied to a piece of string or fishing line. Cast your line into the water and wait for the line to feel heavier. This part of crabbing can take a while, so perhaps have a few fun word or I-spy games up your sleeve!

 WHEN YOU FEEL a pull on the line, carefully raise it and you should find one or even a cluster of crabs hanging off the bait. Pick off the crabs, by handling the body of the crab, and place your crabs in a bucket of seawater. Be careful not to overcrowd the bucket because crabs don't like to be in too close proximity – they could start fighting! Place your bucket in a shaded spot so that the water doesn't heat up and there is no glare to upset the crabs.

 THE MOST IMPORTANT thing to remember is when you have finished crabbing to place the creatures back in the sea. These crabs are not for eating, as they must be allowed to grow to full size.

THE COMMONEST CRAB that you will catch is the shore crab, which is mottled brown in colour, although you will occasionally see green and orange ones. Other crabs to look out for include the edible crab, which is the type the fishmonger sells – they are red with shells that look pinched like a piecrust. The hairy crab looks similar to the shore crab but it's easily distinguishable by its hairy legs and shell. The velvet swimming crab has bright red eyes and can give a nasty nip; it's also covered in hairs, but they are finer than those of the hairy crab.

ONE CRAB THAT frequents estuaries instead of the seashore is the pea crab. The male of the species has a pea-sized brown shell. The female looks very different,

 being twice the size of the male, and yellow with a blob of red on its shell. The male is a strong swimmer, whereas the female can't swim at all.

April

Seaside walks

 NORFOLK IS ONE of the most unspoilt and least-populated areas of UK coastline, and with its diverse terrain of sand, dunes, saltmarsh and shingle it's a haven for wildlife and plant life. Here are a few of Norfolk's seaside highlights.

THE NATIONAL TRUST reserve at Blakeney Point has a 3.5-mile-long spit of shingle and sand, which curves out to sea. On the tip of this spit lives the UK's largest colony of seals, with grey and harbour seal as the two resident species. April marks the beginning of the seals' breeding season.

GROUND-NESTING BIRDS ARE also abundant from April, including Meadow Pipits and Skylarks. Be careful where you walk and keep dogs on leads.

April

THE DUNES AT Holkham are worth a visit at any time
of year. The shifting sands make for a constantly
changing landscape – there are sand islands that were
formed in the last 40 years, while deep sand ridges will
disappear overnight after a storm. Dune vegetation is
abundant here, with couch grass, sea sandwort, sea
holly and marram grass, which together are home to
a thriving population of rabbits and birds. Ringed
Plovers and Oystercatchers build their nests here, while
butterflies, such as Common Blue, can be seen flitting
about. Orchids and forget-me-nots also grow here.
The saltmarshes, once the playground of a young Lord
Nelson, with their drifts of sea lavender make for a
spectacular sight. They're alive with birds, some rare,
including Redshank, various warblers, Little Bittern
and White-tailed Eagle.

THE MUDDY MOUTH of Wells Channel is the perfect
place to spot wading birds, such as Curlews and
Oystercatchers as they dip their long beaks into the

mud while foraging for lugworms and
small shellfish. Other birds, such as Knot,
Dunlin and Redshank, scour the surface
of the mud for tasty morsels, such as
mussel larvae.

Seaside stories

Piers

FOR THOSE WHO simply wish to admire the sea views and take in the saline air, an amble along the pier is a perfect way to pass a sunny afternoon.

THE ARCHITECTURAL EQUIVALENT of a daddy-long-legs, the first pier to be built on UK shores was in Ryde on the Isle of Wight. First opened in 1814, of wood construction, it still stands today, but now boasts a more robust iron structure. Iron piers, such as those at Southport in Merseyside and Southend-on-Sea in Essex, were first built in the mid to late nineteenth century.

AS SEASIDE RESORTS grew in popularity, one pier per resort was simply not enough, hence the West Pier – destroyed by fire in 2003 – and the Palace Pier at Brighton. And you can't throw a pebble without hitting a pier in Blackpool, which boasts three of them.

CLEVEDON PIER IN Somerset was once described by English poet John Betjeman as 'the most beautiful pier in England'. It is the only Grade I-listed example still standing.

SOUTHWOLD PIER IN Suffolk was originally built in 1900 and restored in the early part of the twenty-first century after suffering occasional storm damage, on top of mine blasts during World War Two. It houses the usual penny slot machines but it's also home to a curious collection of automata. It is also used as a landing point for the UK's only seagoing paddle steamer, the PS *Waverley*.

OPENED IN 1868, Blackpool Central Pier was once famous for its open-air dances, but it's now renowned for its family-friendly amusements, including a 39-metre-high big wheel.

SOUTHEND-ON-SEA PIER IN Essex is the world's longest, stretching 1.34 miles into the Thames Estuary. A major fire at its head in 2005, damaging the railway station, pub and various shops, caused the pier to be shut off to the public for over two years, reopening on 1 December 2007.

SWANAGE PIER IN Dorset was constructed in the late nineteenth century and is known for its remarkable curve. An underwater camera can be found at the pier's tip so you can view the goings-on in the murky depths, namely eels and marine fish swimming by.

 # Notes

1
....

2
....

3
....

4
....

5
....

6
....

7
....

8
....

9
....

10
....

11
....

12
....

13
....

14
....

April

15
....

16
....

17
....

18
....

19
....

20
....

21
....

22
....

23
....

24
....

25
....

26
....

27
....

28
....

29
....

30
....

May

Wildlife

IF YOU'RE IN the Shetland Isles, Orkneys or Outer Hebrides in Scotland at this time of year, you may get the chance to see whales. From May right through to September you can see minke, long-finned pilot, humpback and sperm whales in the waters around these islands.

LOOK FOR PEELER crabs 'moulting' on the shore – preferably in a place heavy with rock pools. Peeler crabs are so called because their shells regularly fall away, exposing a soft, new shell below. There are restrictions in some areas with regard to collecting peeler crabs, so be sure to read up about this on www.britishseafishing.co.uk before setting out. Peeler crabs can be found under rocks in shallow water – be extra careful when lifting them and replace them in exactly the same spot after doing so, thus leaving the peeler crabs' habitat as you found it.

JELLYFISH BECOME A fixture of coastal waters, particularly in the south, as the sea warms up in the summer months. They are rather beautiful as they propel themselves through the water by ingesting air and blowing it out again. They have a nasty sting, though, and are best avoided, even when washed up on the beach. There are many species that visit the UK's waters. One is the moon jellyfish, which has only a mild sting if you have the misfortune of coming into close contact with it. It is white in colour and translucent, making it difficult to see out of water. It has four pinky-purple circles, like a crudely drawn flower, on its centre. Other species include barrel, lion's mane, compass and mauve, which vary in colour and size, lion's mane being the largest with tentacles trailing up to 30 metres and a bell with a 2-metre diameter. If you get stung by a jellyfish, you will need to apply ice or a cold pack for around a quarter of an hour. Heat will only worsen the pain and some people suffer a delayed reaction up to 10 days after being stung.

DO YOU KNOW what makes those marks on the beach that look like someone has used a piping bag (badly) filled with wet sand? These are in fact coil castings made by lugworms, also known as sandworms. Lugworms are not dissimilar to a garden worm but are black and red in colour, and have pairs of feathery gills along their bodies.

Beachcombing/foraging

Limpets, winkles and whelks

COMMON LIMPETS, THOSE creatures with conical shells that cling to the rocks and seem near impossible to prise off, are in fact rather tasty when cooked. You may think that all that's required is brute force with a spade to remove them from their habitat, but you might end up with a broken spade as they hold fast and refuse to budge. The key to successful limpet removal is to be as quiet as possible as you creep up to them – you might feel a little bit silly when doing this, but the reward outweighs the temporary embarrassment! Once you have reached your crop of limpets, take a small rock and knock the shells. This will dislodge them from the rock. The limpets can be cooked on a barbecue, shells pointed towards the heat. Once cooked, remove the flesh with a pin and devour with a good squeeze of lemon drizzled on top. Another way is to place them in a pot of boiling water for a few minutes, then take them out of the water and extract the flesh from the shells before frying them up with some butter and chopped garlic.

May

WINKLES ARE ANOTHER seaside delicacy that can be foraged with relative ease. They are small with spiral shells, which tend to be dark in colour and look not dissimilar in shape to the garden snail. They are normally found clustered on rocks and are easy to pick off and gather. Place in a bucket of seawater to transfer them to the place where you will prepare and cook them. Wash them and leave them in fresh water with a dash of salt for a good 10 minutes before dropping them into boiling water for a few minutes. You will need a pin and plenty of patience to extract the flesh, but they are worth the effort as they taste delicious, especially with garlic butter or a dash of your favourite sauce.

WHELKS CAN ALSO be foraged. These sea snails are larger than winkles and can be cooked in the same way but they need to be soaked for a few hours and cooked for a longer amount of time. Once you have extracted the flesh from the shell, remove the digestive system towards the rear as these bits can be quite tough and gritty.

FOR SAFETY'S SAKE, only forage at clean beaches, and not when it's too hot, either – for information go to the Environment Agency's water cleanliness page at www.environment.data. gov.uk, which will list the cleanest beaches.

Seaside activities

Rock-pooling

WITH TWO BANK holidays this month and the promise of warmer weather, the seaside is *the* destination for sun-seekers. One popular pastime for those who don't want to stay at home and bake is rock-pooling.

WAIT UNTIL THE tide is at its lowest, when the seashore offers up its secrets in small, glittering pools of water, like miniature salt-water aquariums. Arm yourself with a bucket from the souvenir kiosk and wear shoes with grips on the soles, as the rocks can be slippery and treacherous in places. Be mindful of tide times before setting out – check out the Easytide website (www. ukho.gov.uk/easytide) for up-to-date tide tables – so you don't get caught out by the incoming sea. It is best to pick up any creatures you find very carefully with your hands rather than use a net, and always return your finds to their habitat when you have finished examining them.

WILD TREASURES TO look out for include the edible crab, sea squirts (with two holes resembling a pig's snout) and mermaid's purses, the egg cases of sharks and rays.

SOME OF THE best rock-pooling spots for seashore safaris include:

 WEMBURY BAY IN Devon – a haven for beadlet anemones.

STRANGFORD LOUGH IN County Down, Northern Ireland – where you can find rare Arctic starfish.

HOPE GAP, EAST Sussex, in the shadow of the Seven Sisters cliffs – where velvet swimming crabs can be found.

KILLEDRAUGHT BAY NEAR Berwick-upon-Tweed in Northumberland – where wonderfully named creatures such as the butterfish and bootlace worm can be found.

THE 'BLUE POOL' in the Gower Peninsula in south Wales – which is almost round and doubles as a plunge pool, being 2.5 metres deep.

THANET IN KENT – where the rock pools are alive with piddocks (a type of mollusc), sea anemones and crabs.

Seaside walks

Small islands

THERE IS A liberal smattering of small islands just off the coast of the UK. Some are only cut off by the tide and can be visited on foot twice a day, when the tide is out, while others require a boat ride to reach them. Here are a few islands of note that are great for walking and wildlife:

PIEL ISLAND IS a half-mile ferry ride from the Furness Peninsula in Cumbria, although it can be accessed by foot via a careful walk along the beach from Walney Island at low tide. It is home to a handful of permanent residents and has a smattering of small cottages, a beach (obviously), a pub and a fourteenth-century castle. The island is a haven for seabirds including Black-headed Gull, Herring Gull, Redshank, Greenshank, Ringed Plover, Cormorant, Eider and Shelduck. The views of the Lake District are also impressive.

THORNEY ISLAND NEAR Emsworth in West Sussex is a former Ministry of Defence base separated by a narrow channel known as the Great Deep. You can walk the perimeter of the island but visitors must stick to the signposts as it is MoD land. The island houses an RSPB nature reserve, its salt-water reed beds and undeveloped land making it attractive to Ospreys, Lapwings, Brent Geese, Curlews and Oystercatchers. A seal colony can be spotted at the tip of the island.

May

BROWNSEA ISLAND IS a National Trust reserve in Poole Harbour, Dorset. It's home to rare red squirrels as well as reptiles, such as sand lizards and species of snake, including adders and slow worms. Dragonflies and butterflies are abundant on the heathland. Many migrating wildfowl overwinter here, but at all times of the year you can see waders, including Pied Avocets and Black-tailed Godwits. Sandwich and Common Terns breed in the lagoon in the summer months.

HERM, PART OF the Channel Islands, is only 1.5 miles long by 0.5 miles wide, and is a mix of rocky cliffs, white sandy beaches and tropical-looking turquoise seas. It has one of the most glorious sandy beaches in the UK, Shell Beach, on its north-eastern coast. It's one of the best beachcombing areas, where you can find tiny pink cowrie shells. The rocky cliffs are home to Puffins, Guillemots and Razorbills, and seals can be spotted bobbing on the tide.

Seaside stories

THERE ARE MANY names that crop up time and again to describe different geological aspects of the coast – here is a brief guide to explain what they mean:

Bay

THIS IS WHEN the coastline curves inward with a wide opening, containing the sea. There are many examples, Morecambe Bay being one of the largest.

Firth

THIS WORD COMES from the Norse *fjord*, and describes an estuary or arm of the sea. Examples include the Moray Firth and Firth of Forth, both in Scotland.

Head

DESCRIBES AN AREA of coast that juts out into the sea, and sometimes much higher than the surrounding area, such as Flamborough Head in North Yorkshire, and Beachy Head in East Sussex.

Kyle

THIS IS A Gaelic word describing a sound or a strait (see below). There are many kyles on the west coast of Scotland.

Ness

THIS IS ANOTHER name for a foreland divided from the mainland by a dyke or river, such as Orford Ness, a shingle spit that stretches for miles along the Suffolk coast and is separated from the mainland by the River Alde.

Point

THE TIP OF the land before it gives way to the sea, such as Baggy Point in Croyde, Devon.

Spit

ALSO KNOWN AS a sandspit, this is a narrow bar of sand and shingle sediment, which has built up over time and projects out from the shore. Some spits only appear at very low tides while others are permanent fixtures of the landscape, such as Chesil Beach, which is a shingle spit that connects West Bay to the Isle of Portland.

Strait

THIS IS A narrow body of water, formed naturally, that lies between two land masses and connects two larger bodies of water, such as the Strait of Dover, which is the narrowest section of the English Channel. It separates the UK from the rest of Europe and forms the boundary point between the English Channel and the North Sea.

Notes

1
....

2
....

3
....

4
....

5
....

6
....

7
....

8
....

9
....

10
....

11
....

12
....

13
....

14
....

May

15
....

16
....

17
....

18
....

19
....

20
....

21
....

22
....

23
....

24
....

25
....

26
....

27
....

28
....

29
....

30
....

31
....

June

Wildlife

THERE ARE SOME unusual types of insect to look for in the summer months, starting in June, such as the bee wolf, which sounds like some sort of mythical creature but is in fact a predatory wasp that stalks and kills bees. They can be seen near dunes and sandy heathland, as these solitary creatures dig small tunnels into sand to lay eggs. The Purbeck mason wasp is rarer, and one of its few habitats is the nature reserve at Studland in Dorset. These can be found eating moth larvae on heathland flowers.

SEVERAL SPECIES OF shark, such as blue, frilled and smooth hammerhead, visit UK waters (particularly off the Cornish coast) in the warmer months. The most feared species of all, the great white, has been seen in recent years off the coast of Cornwall, witnesses having described seeing a specimen over 4 metres in length!

DRAGONFLIES CAN BE seen flitting over coastal grassland. Emperor, gold-ringed and common darter dragonflies are some of the more common species to spot.

NEWTS MAY SEEM an unusual sight on the coast, but the great crested newt has been spotted on the dunes on Sefton Coast in Lancashire, along with natterjack toads and sand lizards.

KITTIWAKE EGGS ARE beginning to hatch now. These delicate gulls thrive on the chalk cliffs in Sussex, Yorkshire, the Shetlands and the Orkneys.

A REGULAR VISITOR to the shore at low tide in the summer months is the spiny spider crab. Its size (up to 18 cm in length), spiny shell and orange colour make it easy to spot. It is most common on the shores of the south and west coasts of England. These crabs are on sale at fishmongers, although only the legs are edible.

WEAVER (OR WEEVER) fish swim in the shallows at low tide in the summer months. They are up to 35 cm long and brown in colour. If you have the misfortune to tread on one you could end up with one of their poison-filled spines in your foot, which is immensely painful. The cure for this is to place your foot in the hottest water you can stand to draw out the poison, or to wear sturdy beach shoes when paddling to protect your feet in the first place.

Beachcombing/foraging

Fossils

FOSSIL HUNTING CAN be enjoyed by all ages but it helps to know where to look. Here's a quick guide to set you on the right path.

On the shingle

THE BEACH IS rich in fossils, the foreshore being the best place to spot them and the most easily accessible. Carefully sift the shingle on the foreshore with your fingers. Even beaches without seawalls or cliffs can offer up some treasure, such as the beaches at Charmouth in Dorset, Bognor Regis in West Sussex, Folkestone in Kent and Harwich in Essex. The tideline where seaweed is deposited at low tide is another good place to sift for fossils and amber, especially at Southwold in Suffolk. The low-tide strandline at St Bees in Cumbria is rich with remains of a petrified forest.

Under rocks

SOMETIMES THE BEST fossils are hidden and require you to carefully lift rocks and boulders in order to unearth them. Seatown in Dorset and Port Mulgrave in North Yorkshire are good spots for this.

In cliffs

LOOK ALONG THE cliff face after a high tide for fossils that have been exposed by the sea. Fossils will sometimes poke out of the rocks. Be careful if you are searching at the base of cliffs – wear a hard hat and check for warning signs about falling rocks. The Isle of Wight has some good locations for finding fossils in cliffs, such as at Shanklin and Sandown (Yaverland Beach), where even dinosaur bones have been unearthed, along with fossilised fish and seashells. Not to mention the Jurassic Coast in Dorset, which is abundant with fossils, particularly ammonites.

On scree slopes

ROCK FRAGMENTS AT the base of cliffs, such as those at Hastings in East Sussex, are another rich hunting ground for fossils. Check for warning signs of falling rocks and landslides before you set out. Corals and brachiopods can be plucked from the limestone at Great Ormes Head in Llandudno, Wales, while prehistoric turtle fossils, bird fossils and large sharks' teeth can be unearthed among the rocks at Walton-on-the-Naze in Essex.

FOR MORE INFORMATION on fossil hunting go to www.discoveringfossils.co.uk.

Seaside activities

Visit a tidal pool

 Swimming in the sea can be dangerous due to tidal currents and sudden drops in beach sediment, but one way to enjoy it in relative safety is to swim in a tidal pool. These barnacle-studded, man-made pools are replenished with seawater at each high tide and warm up in the sun, making for a pleasant outdoor swim for all the family. Plus, it can be fun sharing the pool with the odd crab or small fish! Here are some of the best:

Dancing Ledge in Dorset

As the name suggests, it isn't the most accessible on the list, with a clifftop walk and a scramble down sheer rocks to reach it, but the reward of a bracing swim at Dancing Ledge – so called because the water appears to dance as it laps over the uneven ledge – makes the effort worthwhile.

Havre des Pas, St Helier, Jersey

This gracious semi-circular pool, built in 1895, has been restored to Victorian splendour, complete with iron railings and lamps. It boasts a separate pool for toddlers, changing rooms and lavatories. If you're island-hopping, also seek out La Vallette bathing pools, St Peter Port, Guernsey, which date back to the 1850s.

Jubilee Pool, Penzance, Cornwall

THIS TIDAL POOL was constructed at a traditional bathing spot at Battery Rocks. Art deco in design, it was opened by George V in 1935 in the year of his silver jubilee, hence the pool's name. At the time of writing, it is being refurbished.

Tunnels Beaches, Ilfracombe, Devon

THIS TIDAL POOL, built in the Victorian era, is reached through tunnels carved by hand through the high cliffs by miners from south Wales in 1823. These tunnels were wide enough to fit horse-drawn bathing carriages and connected the local town centre to the beach's secluded coves. In Victorian times, the tunnels and beaches were segregated – one for men and one for women; a horn would sound if a man breached the boundary to the women's beach!

The Trinkie, Caithness, Scotland

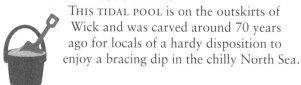

THIS TIDAL POOL is on the outskirts of Wick and was carved around 70 years ago for locals of a hardy disposition to enjoy a bracing dip in the chilly North Sea.

Seaside walks

CEMAES HEAD, PEMBROKESHIRE – this 5-mile walk along the cliffs affords some spectacular birding opportunities, with Cormorants, Fulmars and Guillemots nesting on the ledges of the dizzying 168-metre-high rock. Kestrels and Buzzards swoop overhead and bottlenose dolphins can be seen in the bay. It is also the most popular hang-out for seals on the Welsh coast.

BALNAKEIL BAY TO Sango Sands, Sutherland – one of the many remote beaches in Sutherland, Balnakeil Bay has breathtaking views of Cape Wrath, which often has an impressive dusting of snow. The beach has white sand and is surrounded by headland thick with marram grass. At the entrance to the bay is the now-derelict and rather spooky Balnakeil House, and facing the house on the other side of the road are the ruins of a seventeenth-century church. The mile-long walk to Sango Sands is often bracing on the exposed headland, but it's worth it for the views.

June

DUNWICH TO WALBERSWICK Beach, Suffolk – part of the Suffolk Coast Path, this walk borders Dunwich Forest before reaching Dingle and Westwood Marshes, which are havens for Avocet, Redshank and Lapwing, and many other wading birds and wildfowl. Otters and water voles also reside here, as well as the rarest sea anemone in the UK, the starlet. Westwood Marsh has one of the biggest reed beds in the UK and borders the rugged shingle beach at Walberswick.

ALUM BAY, ISLE of Wight – one of the most appealing aspects of this beach is the ride on the chairlift down the sheer cliffs to the shore, where you can take in the views of the jagged chalk stacks, known as the Needles, and the 58-metre-high Trinity Lighthouse. The bay is also famous for its vast range of colours of sand – from pinks and yellows to whites and browns. Alternatively, walk along the cliffs to Tennyson Monument, with its views across Headon Warren to the Solent and the mainland beyond.

Seaside stories

Formby footprints

FOOTPRINTS ARE THE only things that we should leave behind on a sandy beach because we know that they will be washed away at high tide, but some footprints seem to mysteriously reappear, like the ones on Formby Beach near Southport in Merseyside. Reports of seeing multiple hoof prints in the mud along the foreshore began circulating as early as the 1950s, but, strangely, they would appear on some tides and not appear on others. Other prints would occasionally appear, including bird prints, other animal prints and human footprints, and they looked as though they had been baked hard into the mud. It turns out that these prints are between 4,500 and 7,500 years old. At the end of this 3,000-year period the beach shifted to the west, covering up the prints. In recent years, due to coastal erosion, these ancient prints have been revealed once more.

June

Beach huts

THESE HUMBLE MULTICOLOURED wooden structures
have long been an intrinsic part of the history of
seaside resorts and are a particularly appealing feature
on the UK's beaches – in fact, the seaside would look
underdressed without them. They first appeared in
Bournemouth in the early part of the twentieth century
and were originally old bathing machines with the
wheels removed, employed for the same purpose of
enabling the public to change discreetly into their
bathing costumes before taking the waters. Later,
councils erected small wooden huts not dissimilar to
a garden shed, which could be rented for a small fee
by holidaymakers. After languishing for many years
and considered unfashionable, these structures are
now a status symbol for serious beachgoers, with
some fetching the same amount as a house despite
having little more than a rack on which to hang your
towel. There are around 20,000 of these small wooden
huts across the UK, many of which are now privately
owned and have been 'pimped' by
their owners to include all mod cons.

 # Notes

1
....

2
....

3
....

4
....

5
....

6
....

7
....

8
....

9
....

10
....

11
....

12
....

13
....

14
....

June

15
....

16
....

17
....

18
....

19
....

20
....

21
....

22
....

23
....

24
....

25
....

26
....

27
....

28
....

29
....

30
....

July

Wildlife

FOR SEVERAL WEEKS in summer female bats gather in a maternity roost to have their babies. All 16 of the UK's bat species are declining (they are all protected by law, as are their roost sites), but a dozen of the species can be found in Pembrokeshire in Wales. Playing a busy role in the ecosystem as insect munchers, flower pollinators and seed scatterers, bats are also a valuable part of a habitat's biodiversity.

THE GREATER HORSESHOE bat is the type of bat you are most likely to see around the limestone cliffs and caves of south Pembrokeshire. Their summer nursery roosts include a few caves, with the nursery breaking up in autumn and relocating to cooler climbs.

SIGN UP FOR a bat walk with your local tourist centre and set out to meet the ultimate creatures of the night. Go to www.bigbatmap.org to discover the best places for bat spotting.

WALK THE WHITE Cliffs of Dover (see walks for this month) and along the way you may be lucky enough to witness some unusual sights of nature as you stroll. The chalk grassland on the clifftop path houses many rare plants and insects, including the pyramidal orchid and the Chalk Hill Blue butterfly. Most often seen in bright sunshine, this little summer stunner has shimmering blue wings. When hunting for mates the males can be found in their hundreds hovering just above the ground, forming a spectacular jewel-like carpet.

LITTLE TERNS ARE summer visitors to UK shores. Nesting in small groups on shingle beaches, as its name might suggest, the Little Tern is the smallest tern to be found in the UK. A chatterbox at the best of times, during the mating period it is especially vocal. Fast of flight but short-tailed, its bill is yellow with a black tip. The courtship ritual consists of an aerial display in which the male carries a fish to attract a mate.

Beachcombing/foraging

Lucky glass

SOMETIMES CALLED SEA glass, hunting for these pretty pieces of glass, smoothed of all sharp edges by the sea, can keep children happy for hours. A wonderfully romantic legend to inspire the search is one that children who grew up in Bracklesham Bay, West Sussex, in the 1970s were told by an old lighthouse keeper: lucky glass is gathered and used as bricks by sea fairies to build their palaces.

HARDER TO FIND than ever before – more plastic bottles are used these days than glass – the best hunting spot for lucky glass is on the fringes of shingle beaches. It is said that you should make a wish or pass a piece on to anyone in need of good fortune.

A feather in your cap

COLLECT FEATHERS YOU find on beach walks and use them to create accessories or to jazz up your wardrobe – perhaps a fascinating fascinator or hat for Ladies Day at Royal Ascot, or some unique jewellery, or you could even customise your shoes with feathery fancies?

Looking for lavender

FLOWERING BETWEEN JULY and September, Sea Lavender is a hardy woody plant found in muddy saltmarsh areas. The pretty pinkish-coloured flowers make this a perfect posy for a summer dining table.

Seaside activities

Wild swimming

THIS ROMANTIC-SOUNDING ACTIVITY is purely swimming in open water, be it lakes, rivers or the sea. Swimming in the sea can be dangerous, with unexpected strong currents, hidden rocks, litter and tidal rips. For this reason, it's best to either swim with companions or at least let someone know where you are, or have them wait for you on the shore with a hot drink and a towel.

THE WEATHER MAY be unpredictable, but it is usually safe to assume that the sea off the south coast of England will be warm enough for swimming during the summer months, with temperatures sometimes reaching as high as a balmy 19 degrees Celsius. Coastal waters further north tend to be more bracing but no less enjoyable for a quick dip.

DON'T ALWAYS EXPECT crystal-clear waters. The sea off the south-east coast, for example, always looks a bit grubby. However, this is just sediment, not pollution. From bits of debris shed by the chalk cliffs to muddy shorelines, the sea never looks as sparkling clean here as it does further along in, say, Cornwall. But bathing-water standards are well regulated and many beaches have been awarded a European Blue Flag, demonstrating that they have met the EU's strict water-hygiene standard. Very rarely, and only after significant heavy rainfall, sewage treatment plants may struggle to cope, resulting in raw sewage reaching the open sea.

Swim shoes are worth considering, as most of the
beaches along the south coast are shingle, which can
be extremely uncomfortable to walk on in bare feet.

The health benefits of wild swimming are improved
circulation, a strengthened immune system and a
feeling of being revitalised.

Build a sandcastle

Building sandcastles is one of the best things about
visiting the seaside. All you need is a simple bucket and
spade and a little imagination and you can build your
own kingdom before jumping on it, or watching and
waiting until the tide slowly demolishes it. There is an
art to building the perfect sandcastle and it's all about
the ratio of water to sand, which should be equal
amounts. To do this, you will need a supply of water
on tap while you fashion your creation, and the best
way to do this is to dig a deep hole until you hit water.
Like building a house, you need solid foundations,
so start by making a mound of sand up to a metre
in diameter. Then add towers by filling your bucket
with a mixture of sand and water, giving it a firm pat
with the back of your spade before turning it over and
carefully lifting the bucket to reveal your tower. Use
beach finds, like seaweed and seashells, to decorate
your masterpiece.

From Whitley Bay in Northumberland to Selsey
Bill in West Sussex, many seaside resorts run
annual sandcastle-building competitions. Search for
competitions online or contact local tourist
services for details and then grab a bucket
and spade and dig in!

July

Seaside walks

Cliff-path walks

Whistling Dame Vera's signature tune as
you go, the White Cliffs of Dover in Kent
offer amazing views of the English Channel
towards the French coastline. The best
view of these magnificent high chalk cliffs
is achieved by following the coastal path
towards South Foreland Lighthouse. Used for
defence in both World Wars, physical reminders
of history remain, with slit trenches dug by soldiers in
evidence right the way along the cliffs. You can also
still see the remains of the range-finding station.

Other recommended cliff-path walks include:

The Rhossili Coastal Trail, Wales

Wales at its most beautiful, this walk of 5–6
miles (depending on whether or not you include the
extension out to Worm's Head) follows a path that
mixes dramatic cliffs and a stunning beach,
with plenty of varied birdlife to be enjoyed.

North Antrim Cliff Path, Northern Ireland

A 4.2-MILE WALK to Dunseverick Castle and back, following a clear walkway from Giant's Causeway. Maintained by the National Trust, the views are breathtaking and you'll almost certainly encounter some interesting flora and fauna along the path.

Walton-on-the-Naze, Essex

A 'CIRCULAR' 7-MILE walk that takes you along the cliffs of the Naze and via an embankment above creeks, marshes, mudflats and inlets, the word 'naze' derives from the old English word for nose, relevant to the original shape of the headland. Head across to the Naze Tower (dating back to 1720), and continue north across the grassy clifftop. Take care to note the signage showing where the crumbling cliff edges are.

Seaside stories

Haunted Wheal Coates

LOCATED NEAR ST Agnes, Cornwall, the old tin mine at Wheal Coates goes all the way down to the sea. With waves crashing against the rocks through a grate in the floor of the derelict Towanroath engine house, arguably the most famous industrial building in Cornwall, the mineshaft itself is accessible at low tide through a big cave at the far end of Chapel Porth beach. According to legend, the mine is haunted by many ghosts – the spirits of miners who died while working in grim and dangerous conditions.

Going for gold in Folkestone

IN AUGUST 2014 the Wood family became real-life treasure hunters when they unearthed a gold bar on Folkestone beach in Kent. Kevin Wood, his partner Kirsty and her sister Megan were the first people confirmed to find a 24-carat gold bar, worth £500, which had been buried on the beach by German artist Michael Sailstorfer as part of the Folkestone Triennial arts festival. A total of £10,000 worth of bullion had been buried and gold-diggers filled the beach in a bid to discover the treasure, but the artist cunningly planted a large number of worthless washers too, so as not to give the metal detectorists an unfair advantage.

Cricket that is all at sea

CRICKET ON THE beach is one thing, but a match actually in the sea? Well, technically.

EVERY YEAR TWO sailing clubs race out to the middle of the Solent where they play a cricket match on 'The Brambles' sandbank, which appears only at unusually low tide between Southampton and the Isle of Wight. The sailors from the Royal Southern Yacht Club, Hamble, sail and play against the Isle of Wight's The Island Sailing Club in the annual match which dates back to the 1950s.

WITNESSED BY MANY spectators in boats, who sail out alongside the teams, the entire flotilla waits for the sandbank to emerge from beneath the waves before bowling and batting for a fast and furious half an hour, which is about all they get before the sea floods the 200-metre pitch for another year. Retiring to their crafts, players then sail back to the Isle of Wight for a celebratory dinner.

INMATES FROM PARKHURST Prison on the Isle of Wight were the first to play cricket on Bramble Bank in the 1950s, permitted the brief 'get out of jail' card on account of the fact that they would have struggled to escape.

 # Notes

1
....

2
....

3
....

4
....

5
....

6
....

7
....

8
....

9
....

10
....

11
....

12
....

13
....

14
....

July

15
....

16
....

17
....

18
....

19
....

20
....

21
....

22
....

23
....

24
....

25
....

26
....

27
....

28
....

29
....

30
....

31
....

August

Wildlife

SEVERAL COASTAL BIRDS fly into the UK in August. Look out for vagrant American waders in coastal pools, including White-rumped, Pectoral and Buff-breasted Sandpipers.

BLACK TERNS ARRIVE from breeding on the continent. Look out for these birds with an all-black head and body as they swoop down and snatch food from the water's surface. The Norfolk and Suffolk coasts are the most likely places to spot Black Terns.

YOUNG FULMAR MAY still be spotted making their first flights from cliff nests, as they take 7 weeks to fledge from hatching. Fulmar fly with stiff outstretched wings and can be mistaken for Peregrine when in flight.

STORM PETREL CHICKS are still having night feeds in their nests on rocky islands, particularly off the coasts of Wales and Scotland. The parents resemble black Swallows as they traverse the night sky feasting on plankton.

MEMBERS OF THE Sawbill family, Red-breasted Mergansers (diving ducks with a Mohican-like crest), gather in August in bays and remote rocky coastal areas of Wales and Scotland as they prepare to moult. Flocks of Eider Duck (the heaviest of the ducks that can be found in the UK) might be spotted in tight packs out at sea, which is where they go to moult. Having left their breeding grounds on the Farne Islands, they are most likely spotted off the Scottish coastline.

THE RSPB RESERVE at Bempton Cliffs in East Yorkshire is the perfect place to meet a multitude of wildlife in August. The breeding season for some 200,000 seabirds, hatchings include Grasshopper Warblers, Tree Sparrows, Whitethroats, Sedge Warblers, Skylarks, Linnets and Reed Buntings. Some daytime-flying moths can also be seen, including Cinnabars, Burnets and, if you're lucky, a Hummingbird Hawk-moth. Visit www.rspb.org.uk for more details.

Beachcombing/foraging

Take a pebble dash or dawdle

BEACH STONES AND rocks are fascinating. From plain greys and browns to those housing crystals and those with perfect holes (ideal as pen holders!), start a collection that can be built into a rockery or garden display over time. Read up on the different types of pebbles you can find on the beach (see the guide to stones in February's seaside stories) and then head out to see which you can find.

IF YOU'RE INCLINED to posher pebbles then Camber Beach in East Sussex is one of the UK's best beaches for finding semi-precious stones, but be aware that taking home pebbles from the beach is frowned upon and even illegal in some places, although a memento of one or two pebbles is deemed acceptable – check the protocol for the beach that you are visiting.

Baubles, bangles and beaches

WHITBY JET HAS long since been renowned for its
black beauty, and it looks stunning when fashioned
into jewellery. On the beaches close to the cliffs in
Whitby in North Yorkshire, which is widely regarded
as the gothic capital of the UK on account of its
Dracula connection (appropriate given the blackness
of the stone), finding pieces of jet hidden in the shingle
is not unusual. But do not, on any account, attempt
to scale the cliffs themselves, as they are unsafe for
climbing.

RUNSWICK BAY, JUST north of Whitby, is reputed to
be an excellent spot for unearthing, amongst other
treasures, old coins and semi-precious stones. The
Kent coastline is also reported to be a good
hunting ground for sparkling treasures.
Baltic amber is said to have been found on
these shores.

Seaside activities

Cowes Week

HOP ON A ferry and head to the Isle of Wight for Cowes Week. One of the longest-running and most spectacular sporting events in the UK, traditionally Cowes Week takes place in late July/ early August, just after the Glorious Goodwood horse-race meeting and before the first day of the grouse-shooting season, the so-called Glorious Twelfth (although the dates are sometimes tweaked to ensure the best tidal conditions).

GLAMOROUS, AND ALWAYS a great opportunity for celeb spotting, this world-famous regatta has been running since 1826. It offers lots to do on land, but it is on the Solent and the island's beaches that the main action takes place, with the shoreline offering a ringside seat for spectators.

HEAD FOR A spot between the castle of the Royal Yacht Squadron and the cannons and you'll be perfectly pitched to witness the start and finish of the different races, as well as being within earshot of race officers calling the starts from the castle battlements. Later in the day you can mooch along 'The Green' towards Egypt Point and enjoy the view of the Cowes Week fleet as they finish. Be sure not to miss the fireworks display, which marks the end of the regatta.

Jump off Worthing Pier

THE INTERNATIONAL BIRDMAN Competition is a competition for human-powered flying machines held annually in August in the West Sussex seaside town of Worthing.

FLYERS PARTICIPATE EITHER to raise money for their favourite charities or to have a stab at winning a serious cash prize by designing machines that can actually go the required distance. The big prize of £10,000 is only awarded for the furthest flight in excess of 100 metres.

TO SEE EVERYTHING from fabulous fancy dress to incredible feats of engineering, stake a claim to a spot on the beach close to the pier early, then sit back and enjoy the fun.

What has the Internet got to do with a Cornish beach?

BELIEVE IT OR not, without a cable that runs from a north Cornish beach all the way to New York – a distance of 3,300 miles – the world's Internet would be intermittent at best. The precise location of the beach is under wraps for fear of sabotage, but it's food for thought, when you next find yourself on a beach in north Cornwall, that if you were to dig just 6 metres down while building the trench for your sandcastle you might strike the fibre-optic cable that powers the world's Internet.

Seaside walks

 WALKING ON THE beach in the moonlight is a glorious experience. Several coastal towns host organised walks at night, with some charities also creating fundraising opportunities from nocturnal shoreline rambling. Check with local organisations and tourist information points if you fancy walking at night as part of a group.

See stars in Wales

ALTHOUGH A STEEP climb down the cliff and back again to the car park, at low tide Penbryn Beach in Cardigan is perfect for walking after dark. Start out from the National Trust car park at Llanborth Farm. The walk to the beach takes you via a footpath that goes through the woods of a valley and covers approximately three-quarters of a mile. Once on the beach the sands offer a walk of approximately a mile. Go barefoot and enjoy the feeling of the soft gold sand beneath you while gazing up at the stars.

NOBODY SHOULD RELY on a lucky star when walking at night, so make sure you take a friend, a torch, a basic first aid kit and a fully charged mobile phone.

Wildlife spotting at dusk on the Welsh coast

THE NATIONAL TRUST-OWNED Penbryn Beach in Cardigan is also an exciting place for wildlife spotting at night. Choose a clear night and walk from the car park through the woods to the beach. Look out for Barn Owls on the way, as they hunt for mice and voles. Seals can be seen popping their heads above the water and bottlenose dolphins often play in the bay, but if you're out of luck, you can always spread a blanket on the sand, stretch out and enjoy the view of the heavens – the Milky Way is particularly clear from here.

The Golden Mile in Blackpool

AUGUST IS A great month to take this iconic walk at night. With the tourist season in full swing, embrace the bustling atmosphere and balmy evenings as you follow the Golden Mile (it's actually 1.7 miles between the North and South Piers). Drink in the sights of the illuminated Tower, Pleasure Beach and seaside tourist outlets as you saunter.

TO EXPERIENCE THE full 'fairground' feel of the town, start walking at dusk, then reward yourself with a fish and chip supper, eaten on the prom. With a stick of rock for pudding!

Seaside stories

Benjamin Grey

THE WEST SUSSEX town of Littlehampton was so well loved by Benjamin Grey, who was born in the town in 1838, that he founded a town of the same name in Australia! Grey and his family set out for Australia in search of adventure, eventually settling in the Adelaide hills. Naming the spot after the home he left behind, Littlehampton-down-under is now more than 150 years old!

Brighton's ill-fated West Pier

DESIGNED AND ENGINEERED by Eugenius Birch to attract visitors, the West Pier opened in 1866. A structure built using cast-iron threaded columns screwed into the seabed, reinforced with ties and girders, additions were made over the years, with building finally completed in 1916. A magnificent example of seaside architecture, people flocked to Brighton to visit it.

IN LATER YEARS the West Pier featured in Richard
Attenborough's classic film *Oh! What a Lovely War*,
but sadly, due to safety reasons, the entire structure
was closed in 1975. After that many attempts were
made to source funding for its renewal, but on 29
December 2002 fate intervened, when a fierce storm
caused the south-east corner of the pier's Concert Hall
to collapse. In 2003 two separate arson attacks left the
pier nothing more than a skeleton.

BUT WHILE THE West Pier will almost certainly never
be restored to its former glory, planning permission
has been granted to build an observation tower.
Designed by Marks Barfield Architects, the creators
of the London Eye, in some way at least this splendid
monument will once more provide an impressive focal
point on the west side of one of the
UK's most popular seaside towns.

 # Notes

1
....

2
....

3
....

4
....

5
....

6
....

7
....

8
....

9
....

10
....

11
....

12
....

13
....

14
....

August

15

16

17

18

19

20

21

22

23

24

25

26

27

28

29

30

31

September

Wildlife

ARCTIC TERNS PASS by our coasts on their pole-to-pole migration in September, so you may be lucky in spotting some in transit. This bird is white apart from a black marking on the top of its head, resembling a black cap. Making the longest journey of any bird in the world, some may nest within 700 miles of the North Pole and still get as far south as the Antarctic continent by the end of the year.

ALL FOUR SKUA species – Arctic, Great, Long-tailed, and Pomarine – begin their southbound migrations in September. A good vantage point is had from beaches close to Grangemouth in Scotland, such as Aberdour Black Sands. Similar to large, brown gulls but with longer central tail feathers, skua are hawk-like and prey on smaller seabirds, either killing them or forcing them to give up any food. Big, bold and aggressive, a Great Skua will force down a Whooper Swan and kill it.

CURLEW SANDPIPERS AND Little Stints, two of the small waders now on passage south, can be found singly or in tiny groups all along the east coast of the UK. Look out for them at beaches close to Cresswell Pond in Northumberland. As they are often in the company of the common Dunlin, it's a good idea to carry identification pictures.

PROBABLY YOUR LAST chance of the year to see whales in the UK, Scotland is the best place to spy these majestic creatures. Minke whales can be sighted along the east coast of the Shetland Islands, the Pentland Firth, the Orkneys and the Outer Hebrides, while long-finned pilot whales can be seen in the Minch Strait between north-west Scotland and the Outer Hebrides.

Beachcombing/foraging

Treasure hunting

ONCE THE HOLIDAYMAKERS have packed up and departed, the beach is a great place to try your hand at metal detecting. The best time to hunt is when the tide is out, so the acquisition of a local tide timetable is essential. Most jewellery lost on beaches happens as a result of people swimming in the sea. When fingers contract due to the cold temperature of the sea, rings and bangles are likely to loosen and slip off and chains and necklaces get broken if bathers are swimming energetically. Start at the shoreline and work backwards.

THE TREASURE ACT came into force in 1997 and relates to finds made in England, Wales and Northern Ireland. The Department for Culture, Media and Sport have a leaflet called 'The Treasure Act, Information for Finders of Treasure' and anyone seriously considering taking up treasure hunting must familiarise themselves with this.

AND IF YOU think your chances of finding anything are remote, let Merlin Cadogan persuade you otherwise. Mr Cadogan waded into the sea at Westward Ho! with his metal detector and found an 18-carat nugget. He could scarcely believe his luck when he pulled out the whopping lump of gold.

FOR FURTHER DETAILS on treasure hunting visit www.ncmd.co.uk.

Pennies from heaven

BEACHES ARE AMONG the best places to find old coins. Quite often the finds will be from the Victorian era, when beach holidays first became popular, but occasionally more valuable pennies can be found. A hoard of 900 silver coins were found recently on a beach in Anglesey dating from the thirteenth and fourteenth centuries. Where the English Channel meets the North Sea off Kent, hoards of silverware and Baltic amber have been unearthed.

Seaside activities

FOR THOSE WHO need to get the blood pumping on a day out and a stroll is simply not enough, there are all sorts of high-energy coastal sports to try your hand at, such as:

Skimboarding

THIS SPORT IS similar to surfing in so far as you have a board to balance on, but you start off by standing on the shore to catch a wave rather than paddling out to sea. Standing on the finless board, the skimmer must wait for the water to come in before gliding out to sea towards an oncoming wave and riding it back to shore. Expert skimboarders can perform tricks in the wash of the waves similar to those done on a skateboard, such as 'ollies', in the wash of the waves.

Coasteering

THIS IS ONE for adrenalin junkies with a head for heights and deep water. It's a relatively new activity, pioneered by a group of Pembrokeshire-based surfers in the 1980s, who took scrambling over rocks a step further, by jumping off cliffs and into the sea. The sport is a blend of exploring caves, shore-scrambling, wave-jumping and cliff-jumping. It's also known as 'extreme rock-pooling' as you get to experience aquatic wildlife at close quarters – something that you can't experience on a ramble! As this is a high-risk sport, it's not recommended without the guidance of an expert.

Kitesurfing

THIS SPORT IS for those who are good at balancing and have good upper-body strength. Kitesurfing, like windsurfing, harnesses the power of the wind. The surfer is strapped (though not always) to a wakeboard or surfboard and holds onto a power kite to propel themselves across the waves. Something similar can be enjoyed on land with a skateboard and power kite, or even a sit-down board and kite. Recommended kitesurfing schools are based all over the country, with each running their own courses. If it's something that you have an urge to try then visit the British Kitesports Association at www.britishkitesports.org for details of everything from lessons to kit and terminology to competitions.

Paddle-boarding

DATING BACK TO the 1950s when Hawaiian beach boys stood on their boards while teaching tourists to surf, stand-up paddle-boarding first became popular in California before going global. The sport entails standing on an oversized surfboard and propelling yourself through open water with a single paddle. A great form of exercise for building core stability and improving arm and leg muscles, it's also great for improving balance. Now the UK's fastest-growing water sport, it's better to try it out when the beaches are quieter. For details of courses and lessons visit www.bsupa.org.uk.

Seaside walks

Dog walks

NOT ALL BEACHES are dog friendly, so if you want to take a leisurely stroll with your four-legged friend then seek out beaches where you'll be most welcome.

PADSTOW BEACH IN Cornwall welcomes woofers and offers a long enough stretch to give your dog a good run. It's also extremely beautiful, boasting gorgeous golden sands. It's a little out of the way, which makes for a peaceful amble.

BETWEEN CHRISTCHURCH AND Highcliffe in Dorset you can find Highcliffe Castle Beach. This beach is dog friendly all year round and is a super sandy space that can be reached via the castle grounds. Sheltered and a safe swimming area, both walkers and their canine friends can enjoy a doggy paddle.

ANOTHER BEACH THAT allows dogs, at least in certain areas, is Holkham Beach in Norfolk.

COUNTY ANTRIM IN Northern Ireland is also dog friendly. There are several beaches that encourage dog walking, including Whiterocks Beach in Portrush, and the beaches at Ballycastle and Waterfoot.

RESPONSIBLE DOG OWNERS won't need reminding that they should always clean up after their pooch and keep it from canine crimes such as picnic thieving and shaking their sea-sodden fur all over other visitors to the beach. If in doubt as to whether or not a beach you wish to visit is dog friendly, contact the local tourist information service.

Seaside stories

Smugglers and pirates in north Wales

WHEN IS A smuggler not a smuggler? When they're a pirate, of course! But in fact they were pretty much the same thing, with those involved in either trade happy to smuggle or seize, depending on how much money they could make.

FAMOUS WELSH PIRATES like Black Bart Roberts and Howell Davis seldom sailed in home waters, but many others did. Doing their villainous deeds all around the Welsh coast, these scoundrels viewed north Wales in particular as a smugglers' paradise, especially around beaches that were out of the way and easy to land on, like those at Ynys Môn (Anglesey) and on the Llyn Peninsula.

THESE SMUGGLERS TOOK advantage of the fact that back then the Isle of Man was not officially part of the UK, and so therefore an ideal location for storing contraband, including brandy, sugar and salt. They would then smuggle their goods over to Wales and sell them to the highest bidder.

SAID TO HAVE been constructed by John Lucas of Port Eynon, who organised smuggling gangs on the Gower Peninsula, the Culver Hole cave was another ideal hidey-hole for the spoils and booty of smuggling. Nestling in a rocky crevice, and reached from the cliffs above via a stone staircase, legend also suggests that Lucas created a secret passageway to his 'salthouse' on the opposite side of the cliffs (salt was a valuable commodity at the time). Reputed to have become so wealthy on the proceeds of the illicit goods he smuggled into the country from Europe, the cave and salthouse were parts of the fortress that Lucas built to protect himself from the excisemen.

 # Notes

1
....

2
....

3
....

4
....

5
....

6
....

7
....

8
....

9
....

10
....

11
....

12
....

13
....

14
....

September

15
....

16
....

17
....

18
....

19
....

20
....

21
....

22
....

23
....

24
....

25
....

26
....

27
....

28
....

29
....

30
....

October

Wildlife

GREY SEALS FOUND on the UK coast account for half the world's population. In autumn, females gather at 'rookeries' (pupping sites) on many stretches of coast between the Isles of Scilly in the south-west, moving clockwise across the top of the UK, to Donna Nook in Lincolnshire. The biggest rookeries are in the Inner and Outer Hebrides, the Orkneys, the Isle of May, the Farne Islands and Donna Nook itself.

SEAL PUPS HAVE a birth weight of only around 14 kilograms, but thanks to the fat content of their mother's milk these fascinating creatures soon pile on the blubber that is essential for maintaining their body temperature.

THE UK IS home to two species of seal: grey and common. The most obvious difference is in the shape of their faces: greys have a longer muzzle and their nostrils are parallel; the common seal has a shorter muzzle and nostrils that are V-shaped.

ONE OF THE best places to spot seals is from the deer park that overlooks Jack Sound and Skomer Island at the end of the Marloes Peninsula in Wales. Using the two coves on the headland to raise their young from the end of August to the end of December, this spot is perfect to view seals. Other seal-spotting opportunities can be found at Blakeney in Norfolk, the Orkneys, Farne Islands and Cornwall.

THIS IS THE month to catch sight of Pink-footed Geese, with more than 300,000 arriving from Iceland. The north Norfolk coast is an excellent place to see these birds, who feast on sugar-beet tops left over after harvesting.

ABOUT HALF OF the world's entire population of White-fronted Geese (i.e. some 13,000 of 26,000) winter on Islay in West Scotland, with another 7,000 or so heading for the Wexford Slobs in Ireland, having bred in Greenland or Iceland. Look out for their orange-yellow beaks.

SANDWICH, COMMON AND Arctic Tern can still be spotted in October. The best places to observe these birds are in harbours on the south and east coasts, where they begin their incredible 6,000-mile journey south.

AT HARBOURS IN the south and east of England and around Ireland you may well see Brent Geese as they start to arrive in the UK from their Arctic breeding grounds.

Beachcombing/foraging

Cowrie shells

COWRIE SHELLS – or 'sea cradles' as they are sometimes known – are a rare find on UK beaches. Pink in colour and very pretty, there are just two types of cowrie to be found in the UK: *Trivia monacha*, which has three spots on its top, and *Trivia arctica*, which is plain.

COWRIES ARE VERY small, seldom bigger than a little fingernail and a maximum of 1 cm long. Originally housing a small sea snail, long since deceased by the time the tide washes the shells up on the beach, the best cowrie hunting grounds are below rocks and cliffs and along the fringes of the shingle where they are often hidden among other shells and pebbles.

FOUND MAINLY ON the west coast of the UK and around Ireland, findings have also been reported in Dorset, Sussex and Hampshire.

October

AROUND THE WORLD cowries have cultural traditions attached to them, and here in the UK it is thought that British seafarers of a few hundred years ago used to take them on voyages to trade abroad.

OCTOBER IS AN ideal time to hunt for cowries – when the tourist season has finished. Given their size, a magnifying glass is a useful tool to take with you.

Rubies in the sand

VISIT RUBY BAY near Elie in Fife, Scotland, on a sunny day and it's not just the sea that will be sparkling. The beach has gravel sediment, but look closer along the low- and high-tide lines and you will see tiny bright red garnets shining bright as rubies. These 'Elie Rubies' can also be seen embedded in the solid volcanic rock that makes up the shore. Another spot to find 'rubies' in Fife is at Kincraig Cliffs near Earlsferry, where purple-coloured stones have been found.

Seaside activities

Stone balancing

FOLLOW IN THE footsteps of sculptor Andy Goldsworthy and artist Adrian Gray and see how many stones you can balance on top of each other to create your own temporary monolithic artwork. It requires discipline and impressive balancing skills as no adhesives or supports of any kind are permitted. The stillness and concentration required is akin to meditation; artist Adrian Gray explains the process as listening with his fingers in order to find stillness and balance to create these seemingly gravity-defying artworks. Look on www.stonebalancing.com and be inspired.

Catch your drift

DRIFTWOOD CAN BE transformed into fantastic craft projects. Heart-shaped wall hangings, picture and mirror frames, garden sculptures, mobiles, tea-light holders – a quick Internet search brings up hundreds of ideas. Perfectly smoothed down by the sea's ministrations, the shapes, texture and general appearance of ocean-battered wood is beautifully natural.

THE OPTIMUM TIMES to find driftwood on the beach are early morning and late afternoon, after a storm, or at low tide. If there's a lot of washed-up debris to root through you may find that a sturdy pair of gloves comes in handy.

Shooting gallery

EVEN IF YOU'RE not a naturally talented photographer, the relatively empty autumn beaches make for a brilliant experimental platform. The light in October can offer a beautiful backdrop and, with fewer people about, the opportunities to focus on subjects or expanses are plentiful. Charge up your phone or camera, pick a beach that appeals as a location for your snappy endeavours, then SHOOT! Snap away and play with different features on your camera.

Seaside walks

In the sand prints of the stars

UK BEACHES HAVE often been used as locations for films and TV shows and when walking in the wake of movie stars it's easy to see why these particular shores were chosen. Whether selected for their remote location, dramatic scenery or quintessential British charm, TV- and movie-set saunters are a lovely umbrella theme for a series of walks that can be spread out over the years.

CHANNEL YOUR INNER Bond or M as you walk in the footsteps of Pierce Brosnan on Penbryn Beach in Ceredigion. A location for *Die Another Day*, in the movie the beach is passed off as North Korea! A breathtakingly beautiful beach, owned by the National Trust, Penbryn Beach is also famous for being almost entirely unspoilt by light pollution. Walk in the late afternoon and take a flask of soup for supper and then watch the celestial stars come out.

FEATURED IN THE classic gangster movie *Get Carter* over 40 years ago, the East Durham coastline was so grotty that it earned itself the nickname 'Black Beaches'. Fast forward a few decades, however, and it has cleaned up its act considerably. Now the recipient of a natural beauty award, bestowed by a prestigious European body, the 12-mile stretch of cliffs and sand between Hartlepool and Sunderland is a far cry from the ecological disaster zone that had suffered from over a century's worth OF WASTE-TIPPING FROM nearby pits.

BARRY ISLAND WAS one half of the setting for TV comedy hit *Gavin and Stacey*. Complete with promenade, funfair and Marco's cafe, the Vale of Glamorgan town and beach enjoyed a surge in visitor numbers following the popularity of the series, especially the sandy beaches of Whitmore Bay. Don a kiss-me-quick hat and recall the show's funniest moments while you walk.

POTTER OFF TO Freshwater West beach on the Pembrokeshire coast and see the location for Shell Cottage of Harry Potter fame. Set designers recreated the cottage belonging to Bill Weasley and Fleur Delacour here, which is in Cornwall in the books.

RUN ALONG ST Andrews West Sands Beach in Fife, where one of the most famous scenes in *Chariots of Fire* was filmed. Supposed to be Broadstairs in Kent in the movie, the actors were filmed running on the

2-mile stretch of wet sand. The beach holds a Blue Flag, while the movie went on to win an Academy Award for Best Picture.

Seaside stories

Songs of the sea

WHAT SHALL WE *do with the drunken sailor,*
What shall we do with the drunken sailor,
What shall we do with the drunken sailor,
Earl-y in the morning!

Way hay and up she rises
Way hay and up she rises
Way hay and up she rises
Earl-y in the morning

WE ALL KNOW sea shanties like 'Drunken Sailor' and 'Bobby Shafto', but where do these songs of the sea stem from? Believed to be the core entertainment on board ships in the past, music surely cheered up long spells on the ocean waves for sailors and fishermen.

THE BEAT OF these songs was also useful, as sailors undertook tasks to the rhythm of the ditties. Pulling line, raising or trimming sails, weighing anchor, and even the tedious and repetitive job of manning the bilge pumps were all done 'in time' and more enthusiastically when such tasks were set to music.

As well as songs to work to there were also more melancholy ballads, usually sung when the anchor was dropped and the crew had partaken of a few drinks. Often describing the harsh conditions of life on board, the songs also told of the lives and loves the men had left behind on land.

But not all sailors had the luxury of singing. In Nelson's navy, songs were not permitted and instead men had to make do with chanting a chorus of numbers or the playing of a fiddle or fife.

The first documented sea shanties were a collection of songs composed to celebrate the defeat of the Spanish Armada, but what of the name – where did 'shanty' come from? Some say that it derives from the French *chanter* ('to sing') while others claim that the word comes from the English word 'chant'. Either way, along with the songs still being sung at sea today, the sea also continues to inspire singers and musicians the world over and across all musical genres.

 # Notes

1
....

2
....

3
....

4
....

5
....

6
....

7
....

8
....

9
....

10
....

11
....

12
....

13
....

14
....

October

15 ....

16 ....

17 ....

18 ....

19 ....

20 ....

21 ....

22 ....

23 ....

24 ....

25 ....

26 ....

27 ....

28 ....

29 ....

30 ....

31 ....

November

Wildlife

MANY AREAS AROUND the UK coastline have bird observatories where you can get the best out of your birdwatching experience, and November is a great month to take advantage of these.

IF THE WEATHER is fair then Fulmar will now return to breeding cliffs around the coast (if it gets fiercely windy they fly back to the open sea until the wind dies down a bit). You'll hear them before you see them if they have taken up perches in the cliffs, as their breeding display combined with the greeting and grouching that goes on between them is a very noisy affair.

PIED AVOCETS, WITH their long, thin, upturned beaks and black-and-white plumage, have not entirely deserted their breeding grounds, which are found mainly on the east coast from The Wash in Norfolk to the Isle of Sheppey in Kent. Harbours on the south coast also host small numbers during the winter months.

FORTY MILES WEST of Oban, the Isle of Coll in the Inner Hebrides is always a wildlife-watcher's paradise, but in November it becomes a 'full house' with vast flocks of Barnacle, Greylag and White-fronted Geese settling on the island. Otters are also regularly spotted here, with dolphins, whales and porpoise scooting around the island's waters, too.

Beachcombing/foraging

Crafting with flotsam and jetsam

WITH THE FESTIVE season looming, November is the month to stock up on natural resources for a major Christmas craft fest. Decorations, cards and gifts can all be made from flotsam and jetsam. Take a bag and your imagination and go on the hunt for nature's creative components. Lucky glass (sea glass), pottery, feathers, shells, pebbles, driftwood and dried seaweed can all be used to make everything from jewellery to festive wreaths – look on Pinterest to see the extent of what even the most novice crafter can achieve.

Seaweed harvest

NOVEMBER IS YOUR last chance of the year to forage for rock samphire, sometimes called sea fennel or sea asparagus. Local to the south and west coasts of the UK (and not to be confused with marsh samphire, in season in summer months and not nearly so tasty), rock samphire has flat heads of yellowish flowers and long, fleshy leaves. Emitting a strong but not unpleasant aroma when crushed, the taste is sweet and reminiscent of carrots.

GROWING IN NOOKS and crannies of rocks, often in the highest parts of cliffs, getting hold of the stuff can be tricky, and although it's tasty, it's not worth risking life and limb for. That said, it can also be found in lower rocks and on shingle beaches. And while it may be at its best earlier in the year, this last batch just means you need to pick only the fresh young growth, avoiding the older, more stringy and woody stalks. In the name of sustainability, do ensure that you take just a few stems from each plant.

ON MENUS SINCE the year dot, this ancient delicacy is enjoying something of a renaissance, with several celebrity chefs featuring it in recipes. However, the simplest – and most delicious – way to cook and serve it is by steaming it and coating it in best-quality butter.

Seaside activities

Visit the RNLI

VISIT A LIFEBOAT station. The Royal
National Lifeboat Institution, funded
entirely by charitable donations, has
been saving lives at sea since 1824.
The 24-hour search and rescue service
operates from 236 lifeboat stations
around the UK and Republic of Ireland,
and all stations welcome visitors. Look online to find a
station and plan your visit. Stations are split into three
categories for visitors: Discover, Observe or Explore.
Whichever you choose, you will be assured of a warm
welcome and a fascinating insight into the work of
these seafaring heroes. Look at www.rnli.org for full
details.

Scavenger hunts

A BEACH-BASED SCAVENGER hunt is a terrific family
activity, which is especially good for children who
have been cooped up inside and who need to burn
off some energy. Make a list of about ten items that
everyone has to hunt for and which can be found
within a 500-metre radius of your location. But make
it interesting by making it specific. For example, a list
might read:

 A SMALL WHITE pebble no bigger than your
middle finger nail

 A PIECE OF brown lucky glass

 AN ICE-LOLLY STICK

SOMETHING THAT IS red

 A PIECE OF rope or string

 A SHELL THAT houses a creature

 A FEATHER

 A PIECE OF seaweed that resembles ribbon

 SOMETHING A FAIRY could wear as a hat

 A PIECE OF wood that you can dig with

GIVE EVERYONE 30 minutes to find as many items as they can and return to 'base'. The person who has collected the most items and (in the event of a tie) in the fastest time is the winner and gets to do a lap of honour of the beach before being treated to chips at the nearest cafe!

Seaside walks

Lighthouse walks

AT THE VERY eastern tip of Anglesey, Penmon Point lighthouse is the focal point of a lovely coastal walk. To the sound of the lighthouse's foghorn, which sounds every 30 seconds, wander along a pretty, award-winning pebble beach, casting your eyes seawards in order to catch sight of seals or porpoises.

A HEARTY 6-MILE walk of a particularly beautiful stretch of North Sea coast just 15 minutes' drive from Sunderland, the magnificent sight of Souter Lighthouse is just one treat to be savoured on this walk along The Leas. Towering above craggy rocks (you can see nesting seabirds at low tide), the striped lighthouse is not only a landmark, it was the first lighthouse to be powered by electricity (in 1871). Although it has been decommissioned, you can visit the engine room and the keeper's cottage, and clamber up the 76 steps to see the view – well worth the effort – from the top.

LOCATED IN THE north-east corner of Wirral, the seaside resort of New Brighton has benefited from a £60 million redevelopment scheme. From the beach here you can view the lighthouse known as Perch Rock, named after its early inception as nothing more than precisely that: a wooden perch. The

structure of the present lighthouse had its foundation stone laid in 1827 but was decommissioned in 1973 and is now a tourist attraction.

Seaside stories

Grin and bare it

SURPRISINGLY FOR A nation so traditionally reserved, there are a number of nudist beaches in the UK. Most of them are on the south coast, but Holkham Beach in Norfolk was once voted one of the best nudist beaches in the country, but was closed to naturists in 2013 following 'unsavoury acts' happening in the sand dunes. However, the western section of Holkham Beach was re-opened to naturists later that year, thanks to lobbying from the British Naturism group. Although open all year round, the bitter North Sea winds that hit the Norfolk coast means that only the very bravest skinny-dippers disrobe in winter.

The radio wreck

THE WRECK OF *Mi Amigo*, the boat that housed Radio Caroline, the most famous pirate radio station of all time, lies on the seabed on the edge of the Black Deep, just off the North Edinburgh Channel in the Thames Estuary.

AN OLD CRAFT that had already enjoyed a full life, on 19 March 1980 *Mi Amigo* broke anchor. The rising tide lifted her and pounded her elderly hull against the seabed, which resulted in leaks springing up in the engine and generator rooms at the stern. After battling with portable pumps for some 8 hours, the crew resigned themselves to the inevitable.

DJs TOM ANDERSON and Stevie Gordon bid listeners farewell, concluding with: 'I'm sure we'll be back one way or another. For the moment from all of us, goodbye and God bless.' After these final words were broadcast, the crew were rescued by lifeboat. Shortly afterwards the ship's lights went out as the sea flooded in and *Mi Amigo* sank below the waves.

 # Notes

1
....

2
....

3
....

4
....

5
....

6
....

7
....

8
....

9
....

10
....

11
....

12
....

13
....

14
....

November

15
....

16
....

17
....

18
....

19
....

20
....

21
....

22
....

23
....

24
....

25
....

26
....

27
....

28
....

29
....

30
....

December

Wildlife

AT HIGH TIDE in December, all around our coasts, you may see (mostly Common) redshanks. There are approximately 60,000 of these birds in the UK. They gather into 'trips' to roost on the same stretch of salting decade after decade.

When feeding, they spread out across upper-shore mudflats and you can easily spot their orange-red legs and beaks. Spotted Redshank, of which there are just around 150 in the UK, are pale and dark grey with longer beaks. The call of a Common Redshank is a quick-fire 'tu tu tu'. The call of the Greenshank is similar, but slower. The call of the Spotted Redshank sounds vaguely like 'tchuit'.

ABOUT 4,000 SCOTERS form small 'rafts' offshore. Although they look black in most light conditions, the males are dark brown. Around 600 of them are Velvet Scoters, which have a white eye-patch and a distinct white speculum (secondary flight feathers that are seen when flying).

OF THE APPROXIMATELY 8,000 pairs of Ringed Plovers that breed in the UK each year, over half this number can be seen on the coast, mainly along the Humber Estuary in north-east England; the Ribble Coast in Lancashire; north Norfolk; The Wash in East Anglia; the Solway Firth, which separates Cumbria and Dumfries and Galloway; and Morecambe Bay, which straddles Lancashire and Cumbria. Nests are very vulnerable as the eggs are not visible on shingle beaches and get trampled on and destroyed. Foxes, dogs and other predators are also threats to these precious eggs.

Beachcombing/foraging

Look what the tide washed in…

THERE IS SOMETHING magical about
the sea, the way it ebbs and flows and
washes up flotsam and jetsam, such as
driftwood, buoys, fishing nets and all
manner of household items – where
does it all come from? Sometimes very
unusual items get washed ashore.

IN 1992 A cargo ship, *Ever Laurel*, carrying 29,000
plastic bath toys had a mishap in the Pacific Ocean
and the entire cargo slipped into the waves. Since
then yellow ducks, green frogs and blue turtles have
been washing up on beaches around the world, from
Hawaii to the Arctic. It wasn't until 15 years after
the incident that they began washing up on shores in
the south-west of England. Apart from having been
on a remarkable journey, these unassuming bath
toys have helped to chart the currents of the
world's oceans.

BACK IN 1997 a goods container filled with millions of Lego pieces toppled off a ship and into the sea 20 miles off Land's End. Ever since then hundreds of pieces have washed up on the beaches of Cornwall and beyond. Appropriately, most of the lost pieces had a nautical theme, so people have been finding the likes of Lego octopuses and life jackets on their beaches.

SINCE THE TIME of disappearing into the sea, the toy treasure could have drifted as far as 62,000 miles, meaning that it could wash up on almost any beach anywhere in the world. In total, 4,756,940 pieces were lost, so the odds of finding a brick or two is not so very unlikely. By taking home any that you find you'll be helping to minimise the risk that these little plastic pieces pose to wildlife.

IN 2008, A cargo of household items, including nappies, perfume and motorbikes washed up in Lyme Bay in Dorset, making rich pickings for scavengers. However, if you do find unexpected treasure on the beach, be it ancient or modern, it is not 'finder's keepers'. Protocol is to declare it to the Maritime and Coastguards Agency, and your honesty may entitle you to a reward.

Seaside activities

Search for a star

THERE ARE 13 species of starfish native to the UK's coastal waters, and they help to balance the delicate ecosystem by eating mussels and barnacles, keeping the hugely populous numbers of these molluscs under control. Starfish have an extraordinary ability to regrow missing arms, even if only a stump of one remains. The best place to discover them (the starfish, not the missing arms) is in rock pools and on the strandline.

SOME SPECIES TO look out for include:

SPINY STARFISH – this species is covered by three rows of spines on each of its five arms. Its greyish-green colour is tipped with purple on its arms and, as one of the larger starfish species, it can grow to 30 cm in diameter.

CUSHION STARFISH – this starfish has short, stumpy arms and thousands of tiny suckers on its feet and is commonly found in rock pools. It varies in colour from olive green to orange and is a diminutive 3 cm in diameter. When it's hungry, it pushes its stomach out through its mouth to surround food!

BLOODY HENRY STARFISH – this species is dark pinkish-red, although you may occasionally come across a purple one. Usually seen on the lowest part of the shore, it dwells in rocky areas of the coast where the waves sweep in. Its size is around 15 cm across.

COMMON STARFISH OR sea star – this species is generally orange in colour, but it can also be brown or purple. Its average size is 20 cm in diameter.

All-weather winter picnics

A FLASK, SOME bread and cheese or perhaps some pre-buttered baked potatoes wrapped in tin foil make for a fabulous feast. Wrapped up warm, sitting on a deserted beach in December and eating good, simple food is life-affirming. Utilising all your senses, smell and taste the natural sea salt of the tide with every mouthful of food, marvel at the sights freely provided by Mother Nature, revel in the soundtrack of the sea and feel the wind in your hair and on your cheeks. And even if the

weather is grim, all you need do is take shelter. Dress for the elements and picnic somewhere sheltered like a promenade bandstand or under a pier.

December

Seaside walks

December dunes

ON A CLEAR and crisp winter's day a walk along the sand dunes evokes a sense of enchantment. Here are some of the best dunes walks:

Aberlady Bay Nature Reserve, East Lothian

THESE DUNES ARE bordered by Muirfield, the world-famous golf course, and there are other points of interest such as the remains of submarines and the chance to spot the roe deer that roam the reserve at dusk.

Saunton Sands, north Devon

BEHIND THIS UNCULTIVATED stretch of sandy beach you will find Braunton Burrows, one of the largest sand-dune systems in the UK. Rich in flora and fauna, a winter walk here will be accompanied by the sound of the crashing sea, as Atlantic rollers rush onto the beach.

Studland Bay, Dorset

MEANDER THROUGH DUNES and heathland behind the white sands of Studland Bay and you'll be forgiven for thinking you have stumbled into paradise. On the northern stretch, easily reached by ferry and with a desert-island feel to it at the best of times, in the bleak midwinter you are almost guaranteed to achieve perfect tranquillity and absolute solitude.

West Wittering, West Sussex

THIS STRETCH OF sand offers stunning views of the Solent and Chichester Harbour, and along with East Head, a remote sand-dune spit, makes for a beautiful walk. Parking is conveniently adjacent to the start of the walk.

Walberswick, Suffolk

CROSS THE BRIDGE that leads from the charming village of Walberswick to the beach and you will discover a ridge of dunes in which to wander. And if you have an artistic eye you'll see for yourself why so many artists set up easels: because the light is extraordinary.

Seaside stories

Dinosaur walks

SOME BEACHES REVEAL incredible secrets dating from prehistory at low tide:

DINOSAUR FOOTPRINTS CAN be seen pressed into the mud at Jackson's Bay, Redcar and at Burniston Bay, both on the North Yorkshire coast. This area was once a large estuary inhabited by three-, four- and five-toed carnivorous and herbivorous dinosaurs. Due to the nature of the rapid erosion of the rock, you could be the first to see footprints formed 160 million years ago.

ANOTHER PLACE TO see dinosaur footprints is at Hanover Point on Brook Beach on the west coast of the Isle of Wight – here you will see iguanodon and theropod prints.

A CLUSTER OF megalosaurus, stegosaurus and cetiosaurus footprints have been discovered at An Corran Bay on Staffin Beach on the Isle of Skye. These prints are on sandstone and are often covered up by the tide and a dusting of sand – the best time to see them is after the winter storms.

Naughty postcards

DATING BACK TO the early 1930s, saucy seaside postcards are as much a part of the UK seaside as candyfloss and stripy deckchairs. A traditional element of any visit to the coast, people sent these cheeky cartoon-style cards all over the world. At the peak of their popularity sales hit a staggering 16 million a year. Full of nudge-nudge-wink-wink innuendo and usually depicting clichéd characters such as doctors, nurses, ladies with large bosoms and suspicious men in overcoats, the *Carry On* films were surely inspired by these cards.

WORRIED ABOUT DECLINING moral standards, in the 1950s the government of the day tried to crack down on saucy postcards, with English cartoonist and postcard artist Donald McGill firmly in their sights. But the 1960s saw the seaside postcard enjoy a renaissance and they continued strongly into the 1970s. By the 1980s, however, sales were on the slide again. Attitudes were changing.

THE POSTCARDS HAVE since been revamped with cartoons and illustrations that are a better fit for the times. Original postcards in mint condition can now fetch high prices at auction.

 # Notes

1
....

2
....

3
....

4
....

5
....

6
....

7
....

8
....

9
....

10
....

11
....

12
....

13
....

14
....

December

15
....

16
....

17
....

18
....

19
....

20
....

21
....

22
....

23
....

24
....

25
....

26
....

27
....

28
....

29
....

30
....

31
....

Index

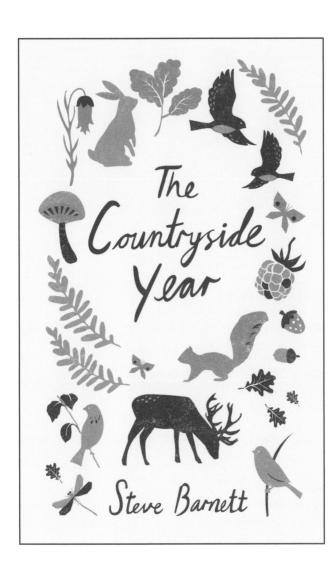

The Countryside Year

Steve Barnett

THE COUNTRYSIDE YEAR

Steve Barnett

ISBN: 978 1 84953 683 7

Hardback

£9.99

This charming and practical handbook is bursting with tips, facts and folklore to guide you through the countryside year. Find out how to identify birds by sight or song, spot animal tracks, name wild flowers, butterflies, insects and trees, and forage for natural foods throughout the seasons.

With handy diary pages for making your own notes each month as you explore the hills, forests and fields, this is a must-have for any lover of the great outdoors.

If you're interested in finding out more about
our books, find us on Facebook at
Summersdale Publishers
and follow us on Twitter at
@Summersdale.

www.summersdale.com